ALSO BY MARIO VARGAS LLOSA

CONVERSATION AT PRINCETON

CONVERSATION

AT

PRINCETON

MARIO VARGAS LLOSA

WITH

RUBÉN GALLO

TRANSLATED FROM THE SPANISH BY
ANNA KUSHNER

FARRAR, STRAUS AND GIROUX

NEW YORK

Farrar, Straus and Giroux
120 Broadway, New York 10271

Library of Congress Control Number: 2022041851
ISBN: 978-0-374-12901-9

Designed by Abby Kagan

www.fsgbooks.com
www.twitter.com/fsgbooks • www.facebook.com/fsgbooks

1 3 5 7 9 10 8 6 4 2

CONTENTS

CONVERSATION AT PRINCETON

INTRODUCTION: MARIO VARGAS LLOSA AT PRINCETON

I met Mario Vargas Llosa shortly after I began teaching at Princeton in 2002. Peter Dougherty, the head of the university's press, had written to invite me to a short meeting: "Princeton is about to publish Mario's essay about *Les Misérables*, and he'll be coming here tomorrow to talk about his book with our sales team," he said in his message.

I attended the meeting, which was held in one of the university's classrooms, and there was Mario, in a suit and tie, surrounded by the publishing house's sales team, men and women in their thirties, forties—all of them American—with that shyness typical of the university set. They never looked you in the eye, they spoke and moved with great trepidation, as if they didn't know how to behave or what type of questions they should ask.

Mario, in contrast, projected a politeness and pleasantness that accompanied him wherever he went. He was relaxed and talked to the salespeople as if they were old friends. When he started to tell the story of his book, his voice and expression lit up the room.

"Just imagine," Mario said. "Victor Hugo is a man who was a virgin when he married. He had never been with a woman before. That was a very rare thing for a man of his time. He was a virgin!"

The agents' discomfort increased considerably. They were taking notes in booklets full of lined yellow paper and were doing everything possible not to look at Mario as he spoke.

"But then," Mario continued, "something unexpected happened. On their wedding night, Victor Hugo enjoyed that new experience so much that he made love to his wife seven times."

The sales agents kept their eyes glued to their notes and wrote more quickly.

"Seven times. Not once or twice, but seven. Seven times in just one night. Can you imagine the amount of energy one needs for that? And he was no longer a young man. Seven times!"

The sales agents blushed as they kept speedily taking notes. One woman went so red in the face that I feared she would explode.

When Mario finished relaying the life of Victor Hugo—his marriage, his love stories, his political problems, his exile on the Channel Islands—the director announced there were a few minutes left for questions.

Following a long silence, the woman who had become red and now returned to a less violent color asked, "How would you classify that book? Biography or essay? It's very important to specify so we can determine its placement in bookstores."

While she asked this, I looked at her and remembered Mario's words, "Seven times! Seven times!"

Mario gave her an answer that seemed to calm her down, and she carefully recorded it in her yellow notebook.

Shortly after, Shirley Tilghman, the university's president, named me the director of the Latin American Studies program. I accepted, and my first project was to invite Mario to spend a semester with us. He had already been a visiting professor at Princeton—and at many other universities in the United States and around the world—but he had not been back since the early 1990s, just after his presidential campaign in Peru.

At Princeton, in addition, was Mario's archive. In the 1990s, the university's library had purchased his correspondence, the drafts of his novels, and many other documents that now fill 362 boxes that hundreds of researchers from around the world have consulted.

Mario accepted the invitation and since then has spent three semesters with us as a visiting professor. On one of those visits—it was fall 2010 and the campus's trees were a fiery red—he gave a seminar on Borges's essays and another about the Latin American novel.

The semester was going along at its usual pace—seminars, dinners with colleagues, trips to New York, where many of Princeton's professors live—when one October day, in the wee hours of the morning, I was awoken by ringing.

I picked up the phone half-asleep.

"Good morning. Forgive me for bothering you so early. I'm Mary, from Princeton's Nobel Prizes office."

I hadn't managed to fully wake up. Nobel Prizes office? I didn't know such an office existed.

"We urgently need to locate Mario Vargas Llosa," the woman's voice told me.

I was shaken awake when I made the link between those two phrases—"Nobel Prize" and "Mario Vargas Llosa"—being used in the same sentence.

I jumped out of bed, showered and dressed as quickly as I

could, and five minutes later, I was on the subway, headed toward Fifty-Seventh Street, where Mario had rented an apartment just steps from Central Park.

When I got to his building, I ran into a crowd of journalists and curious onlookers, armed with TV cameras and microphones, gathered at his door.

Across the street was a florist, and I went in to buy an arrangement.

"Of course," the clerk said. "What's the occasion? A birthday? A wedding?"

"A Nobel Prize," I replied.

I managed—with the floral arrangement in tow—to make my way among the hordes of journalists, take one of the elevators, and arrive at Mario's apartment. The door opened and I found another small crowd there: more TV cameras, microphones, and reporters running back and forth across the apartment from one end to another. All phones—the intercom, landlines, visitors' cell phones—were ringing at once, and there weren't enough hands to answer them.

"Rubén!"

I heard my name called, and then there was Mario, impeccable and with an unwavering serenity in the midst of that Babylon-like ruckus.

"Imagine," he said to me, "the Swedish Academy got in touch before six a.m. I was reading on the sofa. Patricia took the call and went pale before giving me the phone. I got very scared when I saw her, and the first thing I thought was: There's been a death in the family. I took the receiver and a very proper gentleman said that he was from the Swedish Academy, that I'd been awarded the Nobel Prize, and that in five minutes they would publicize the news. He told me that if I wanted to talk to anyone, I should do it right then because

I wouldn't be able to later. I hung up and was left thinking, here on the sofa, about what that meant. Just five minutes later, as they had warned me, the storm began. I didn't get to call anyone."

"Mario, we're ready to shoot," the cameraman from Televisión Española said.

The Nobel storm reached Princeton. A day didn't go by without journalists from all over the world showing up and walking across the university's campus as if it were their own home, even making their way into classrooms where Mario was giving his seminar.

Luckily, Rose, the program's administrator, was an imposing Puerto Rican who, from day to night, became Mario's bodyguard. "*El dotol Vaga* Llosa is not available," she would grunt when an outsider came to the office.

Besides the inopportune visits, the office's phones rang off the hook and the fax machines reeled off page after page. The university mailman had to get a supermarket shopping cart to deliver the pounds of letters and packages that arrived daily.

The faxes and letters contained the most unrealistic requests in the world. Mario laughed like a child upon reading those outlandish entreaties, and we could hear his belly laughs from his office.

"Rose, come here for a minute so you can read this letter," Mario would say.

In a fax—illustrated with graphics and numerical tables— the owner of an ice cream factory in Ayacucho, Peru, addressed Mario as his "illustrious compatriot" and told him about the marvelous business his little factory was, with gains of 400 percent in the previous year. "That is why," the ice cream vendor explained, "I thought of proposing that you invest the Nobel money in my business. This will allow you to triple your capital in two years. You help me and I help you."

"Rose, look at this one," Mario would call from his office.

A brown paper envelope, with stamps from India, came addressed only to "Mario Vargas Llosa, Nobel Prize, United States" and had miraculously arrived at the university. Inside was a sheet written in careful calligraphy and addressed to "Dear Sir." The author told Mario that he'd been awarded the Nobel Prize for being a very good writer but also surely because he was a very generous man. "And as such," the Indian man concluded, "I ask that you send me some assistance taken out of your prize to pay for a stomach operation that doctors recommended to me long ago but that I have not been able to complete for lack of funds."

Not all requests came in writing. One day, the manager of a fashionable restaurant came by the office, saying he wanted to take advantage of the Nobel to bring Latin food to his customers. He had thought of a large banquet of Peruvian food to which all of New Jersey's who's who would be invited. All of this would be presided over by Mario, and "it won't take more than three or four hours of your time: the duration of the banquet."

"*Dotol Vaga* Llosa doesn't like banquets," Rose grunted as she saw the manager to the door.

Four days after the Nobel Prize announcement, Mario had planned a conference, in Spanish, which would go by the title "A Brief Talk on Culture."

The day before the conference, Mary, who was in charge of the Nobel Prize office, called me to emphatically recommend that we move the event to Richardson Auditorium, the university's concert salon, a space that could fit up to five hundred people.

"But the conference is in Spanish," I told her. "Besides, it's about a very specific subject. We have a room that seats a hundred, and I don't think we'll fill it. How many Spanish speakers could there be in Princeton?" I asked her.

"You don't know about Nobel Prize winners," Mary told me. "People want to see them, go up to them, touch them."

We listened to Mary and reserved the auditorium at Richardson.

The day of the conference, we found a crowd pressed up against the entrance. There were five hundred people inside and at least as many outside.

In his talk—which was later published as *The Civilization of the Spectacle*—Mario critiqued Michel Foucault and his concept of freedom, establishing a link between the French philosopher's ideas and the anarchy experienced today in France's public schools. It was a line of reasoning that could be read as a frontal attack on the North American academy, where Foucault's work continues to be, after so many years, a key reference for students and professors. The discussion with the audience, I thought, would be intense.

But everyone in the room listened to Mario's words with smiles that didn't fade. When the moment came for questions from the audience, a long line formed.

"I'm from Iquitos," a gentleman said, very close to the microphone, "and, although I've been in this country for twenty years, I'd like to tell you that the Nobel Prize is an honor for all Peruvians. It is a prize that elevates the name of our country."

"I'm from Lima and I work in construction," shouted the second one in line when his turn came, pushing the microphone away, "but in my free time, well, I write poetry. And I'd like to show you some of my poems, Don Mario."

"I cried," a woman said. "I cried, Mario, when I saw the news about the Nobel on television. I cried because it is a source of pride for all Peruvians, one of the most beautiful things that could happen to us."

When Mario finished signing, a security guard—a blond man in uniform who appeared to be no older than twenty—escorted us off the stage. There were too many people outside, he said, and it would be preferable to use the musicians' exit, which would leave us out behind the building. From there, we could walk to the street, where a car would be waiting for us to take us to the restaurant at which we'd agreed to meet with the novelist Joyce Carol Oates.

We followed the guard, and when we went out the back door we heard, in the distance, the voices of the crowd gathered in front of the main entrance. From out of nowhere, a voice yelled, "There he is," and in one second, the human wave had reached us and completely surrounded us. There were hundreds, thousands of Peruvians crammed onto the campus while that blond security guard, armed with a walkie-talkie, tried to make way for us.

Where had all those Peruvians threatening to crush us come from? Mario told me that in Paterson, a New Jersey town, there lived one of the most notable Peruvian communities abroad and that it totaled more than a hundred thousand.

"Well, it seems that the same hundred thousand have come en masse to Princeton," I thought.

"Mario! Mario! I voted for you," one of the Peruvians shouted as we made our way forward, with difficulty.

"A photo for my *abuelita*," a woman said, approaching Mario while her husband shot the camera.

"Mario, sign this book for me. Write: For Maritza," another girl said as she offered him a pen.

Despite the endless requests for photos and autographs, to which Mario agreed as we kept walking, we managed to advance a few feet. The human masses became denser and denser. At that rate, it would take us hours to reach the street, if we managed to get out of there without being crushed.

There came the moment that Paterson's Peruvians closed off our path. Dozens of hands with books and cameras stretched out before us, and people were yelling, "Mario! Mario!" The blond security guard called on his walkie-talkie to say that we couldn't move forward, that we were trapped.

At that, Mario—who continued to sign books and pose with his fans nonstop—took the lead and made way for us amid Paterson's hundred thousand Peruvians. He walked determinedly as he greeted fans left and right with his eyes, but always facing forward: it was as if he were parting the sea with his gaze. Blondie had stayed behind and was still talking on his walkie-talkie.

When we finally got to the street and entered the university car the chauffeur took off, and we left behind Paterson's hundred thousand Peruvians.

"You got scared," Mario said to me.

"I thought they were going to trample us."

"It was an affectionate audience, but any crowd, even an

affectionate one, can be lethal. I learned that on the campaign trail."

After the Nobel, Mario continued his collaboration with Princeton. The university awarded him an honorary doctorate in July 2014, and he returned as a visiting professor one year later. This time, we decided to teach a class together about literature and politics in Latin America that would analyze how the novel has responded to the great historic events of the twentieth century.

As part of the course, I asked the students to work in Mario's archive at Princeton. They each had to present, to the whole seminar, the documents they had found while doing research. Those presentations were one of the most fun parts of the class. Each week, a student took center stage, connected a computer, and projected his or her discoveries on the big screen.

Lara Norgaard, who in addition to being a student also worked as a journalist for one of the university's papers, found the articles that Mario had published at the age of fifteen about subjects as diverse as tuberculosis in Lima or corruption in the pharmacies. While she exhibited these reports, Mario listened to her, fascinated.

"I had forgotten I'd written that article," he said.

The students chose other exciting subjects: Mario's correspondence with his translators, his time in Puerto Rico in the late sixties, the changes that appear in different drafts of his novel about Flora Tristán.

One day, a student projected a photo of a sheet written in youthful script.

"This is a love poem that Mario Vargas Llosa wrote at the age of twelve," the student said.

"I wrote that poem? How embarrassing!" our guest exclaimed.

There were some very nice moments in which the students, after having learned so much from listening to Mario's talks, dared to show him something—a forgotten detail, a lost text—about his own trajectory: a pedagogic model in which the teaching happened in both directions and that Mario enjoyed with generosity and a good attitude.

Thus, we spent the whole semester: gathering with the students on Tuesday afternoons, listening to the presentations, debating about Trujillo's dictatorship and the Cuban Revolution, about the *nouveau roman* and Sartre's existentialism.

In November, nearly at the end of the semester, we organized Mario's final public appearance before he finished his stay and returned to Madrid. We were coming to the end of a terrible year, one that had begun with a terrorist attack on the magazine *Charlie Hebdo* in Paris and that was concluding with the attack at Bataclan that had occurred just days before, on November 13. We decided that we would devote that last class to terrorism as a threat against the type of intellectual work—based on dialogue, ideas, words—that we wanted to teach our students.

For that meeting, we also invited Philippe Lançon, a friend and journalist at the daily *Libération*, a great connoisseur of Mario's work and one of the wounded during the attack on *Charlie Hebdo*. Philippe traveled to Princeton from Paris—his first trip since that terrible day—and we had a three-way dialogue. He gave us firsthand testimony, telling us in all detail about what he experienced that January day when two young men armed with machine guns entered the paper's newsroom, and during the months he spent afterward at the hospital, recovering from his wounds. In his comments, Mario placed that attack in the wider context of the terrorist threats and reminded us that intellectual life is and has been the best antidote to that type of violence.

The semester flew by: I remember the last meeting with the students, the applause, the sad faces, the affectionate goodbyes with which they bid Mario farewell.

As always, Mario's departure left a great void at Princeton. We missed his passion for literature and for ideas, his radiant presence, his commitment to politics, his warmth and good nature. It was then that I decided to keep working with all of the material we had created throughout the semester— I had fifty hours of recordings, student presentations, notes on everything we had done during the seminar. Little by little this book took shape; it is a testimony to the hours we spent conversing about literature and politics with the students. It is also a way of making Mario's presence continue on at Princeton and in the world.

RUBÉN GALLO

I

NOVEL THEORY

What is a novel and what role does it play? Our conversation at Princeton began with a review of the most important theories about the novel, from social realism to the nouveau roman, *before going deeper into the experience of the Boom and the effect of the great political events of the twentieth century on literature.*

RUBÉN GALLO: I'd like to begin this dialogue with a reflection about the novel, that literary genre born in the Renaissance, which flourished in the eighteenth century and reached its apogee in the nineteenth century with figures such as Dostoyevsky, Tolstoy, Balzac, Dickens, and Pérez Galdós. Ian Watt and other historians have argued that the novel is a bourgeois genre, a literary form that not only was born with the bourgeoisie but also narrates the adventures of bourgeois characters. Would you agree with this characterization?

MARIO VARGAS LLOSA: That is too schematic a declaration about a genre that is so complex and has so many offshoots. It seems more precise to me to say that the novel is born when life goes from being rural to more urban. The emergence of the novel is linked more to the city than to the bourgeoisie.

The rural world produces poetry, but the city foments the development of narrative. That occurs practically the world over. The novel fundamentally describes a city experience, and even the pastoral genre is about an urban perspective. When life is centered around a city, the genre of the novel reaches great development. It is not exactly born with the city, but it is at that moment that narrative becomes popularized and comes to be very widely accepted.

The novel was considered minor within different literary genres. What stood out, of course, was poetry, the creative genre par excellence. Later, through the end of the nineteenth century, what ruled was theater: the performance of works gave an author intellectual prestige. Let's recall the case of Balzac, who became a novelist when he failed at playwriting. We now consider him one of the greatest narrators ever, but he nonetheless felt enormous frustration because he failed as a dramatist. Theater was what afforded great prestige—think of Shakespeare during the Renaissance—and that genre was considered an intellectually superior category.

Novels, in contrast, were aimed at a much wider audience than poetry or classical theater and were considered a popular genre, for less sophisticated and even less educated people. As a matter of fact, in the Middle Ages, the first novels were written to be read in public, on street corners, and thus reach an illiterate audience. They were read by troubadours and acrobats, who entertained audiences with tales of chivalry. It was a minor genre until the nineteenth century, when it began to gain prominence and importance. One of the key authors who gave great prestige to the genre of the novel was Victor Hugo, who was already a great poet, a great playwright, when he suddenly decided to write novels. *Les Misérables* gave the genre extraordinary prestige.

I would associate the novel with urban culture more than with the bourgeoisie. The concept of the bourgeoisie is a very limited, very reductive concept, and the origins of the novel are much more working-class. When the bourgeoisie was just coming into being, there were novels written that reached a wide audience, an audience that in many cases was illiterate but that listened to the stories as told by wandering performers.

SARTRE AND THE *NOUVEAU ROMAN*

RG: When you began writing in the fifties, there were many models for what a novel could be: on the one hand, there was Robbe-Grillet with his idea of the new novel, the *nouveau roman*, that sought to break with the realist model and experiment with new ways of narration. On the other hand, there was Sartre's existentialism, which proposed a politicized vision of narration. From a very young age, you identified yourself with Sartre and not with the experimental authors who followed Robbe-Grillet. How did that debate about the novel reach Peru, and why did you choose the Sartrean model?

MVLL: The interwar period yielded literature with a great commitment to politics: there was an enormous politicization in all of Europe. The literature resulting from that general politicization was deeply linked to social problems. Before Robbe-Grillet's *nouveau roman* came about, there were already two trends: on the one hand, socialist realism, which considered literature as a weapon in the social fight against the established order, as an instrument of change, and as a vehicle for revolution. Marxists and communists defended that conception of literature: realism that should politically educate the masses and push them toward socialism and revolutionary action. In the face of that school, another trend emerged, defended by Sartre and other great writers such as Camus, who said yes, but literature cannot be pedagogical, literature cannot be a political propaganda tool because that kills creativity, literature has to go beyond what is purely political and encompass other human experiences. And thus arose Sartre's thesis, which had enormous influence the world over, from Europe to Latin America. My generation, particularly, was very marked by Sartre's ideas about the novel.

When I read the second volume of Sartre's *Situations*, called *What Is Literature?*, I was blown away by his ideas. For a young man with a literary vocation in a country as underdeveloped as Peru was in those years, Sartre's ideas were very stimulating. Many writers from Peru, from Latin America, from the Third World, asked themselves if in their countries—devastated by terrible problems such as a very high rate of illiteracy, enormous economic inequalities—it made sense to make literature. In his essay, Sartre responded that of course it makes sense to create literature, because literature, besides something that produces pleasure, that stimulates imagination, that enriches sensibility, can be a way of raising the consciousness of social problems in the reading public and in the greater public in general.

The issue of social problems can have a much greater impact when it reaches readers through a story that is moving and appeals not only to reason but also to emotion, feelings, instincts, passions, demonstrating in a much more lifelike way than an essay can what poverty, exploitation, marginalization, and social inequality mean. In a novel, a social problem—let's give the example of someone who, by virtue of belonging to a specific social stratum, has no access to education or economic advancement—can impact a reader without the need for making pure propaganda out of literature, or making it pure political pedagogy. Sartre's theses turned out to be very stimulating: you came to think that, yes, it made sense to write novels in an underdeveloped country, because the novel was not just a way of materializing a vocation but also a way of contributing to social struggles, to the struggle between good and evil from an ethical point of view.

Sartre's theses were very popular all over the world. They seemed much more subtle, much better grounded than socialist realism and opened the possibility of incorporating not just writers who were openly political but also those who, by instinct, out of sensitivity, had conveyed social problems in their novels through their own creativity.

Then, in the late fifties, we saw the *nouveau roman*, a very strong reaction against the notion of socially committed art. Robbe-Grillet said no, the novel does not have to politically educate anyone; the novel is, at its core, an art. Robbe-Grillet opined that "social literature" contained less and less literature and more politics, as proposed in those very entertaining manifestos, which tends to be boring. *For a New Novel*, in contrast, is a very entertaining book that mocks writers who write social novels. Robbe-Grillet proposed experimental art that plays with narrative structures and point of view, that is very careful about language, and that exploits the possibility to create situations of great uncertainty. In this sense, Robbe-Grillet's most accomplished novel is *Jealousy*: there is a narrator, but we do not know exactly what is happening. Someone watches a woman who wanders, and the only thing the reader knows for sure is that there's an element of jealousy behind that constant, maniacal observation. We never discover the identity of that narrator, who is nothing more than an obsessive, maniacal vision, a character who never speaks, who only moves and follows the woman. It's a fascinating experiment that breaks with the finest traditions of the novel. Great novels have always tried to encompass multiple facets of reality and multiple experiences: they are great novels not only because of their literary quality but also because they tell many things and narrate many experiences to paint a portrait of the individual mingling with the masses that are society.

Nathalie Sarraute, who, along with Robbe-Grillet, belonged to the *nouveau roman* movement, published a little book called *Tropisms*, which describes her characters as if they were flowers, moving as a function of the sun, seeking light or moisture. Instead of humans, these absolutely basic, primary beings appear, moving in beats and vegetating like plants. All reason has been abolished in them: they are merely movement, scent, and flavor. These experimental novels depart completely from social-political concerns to affirm that literature is, above anything, an art, a textual construction that generates aesthetic pleasure and that cannot be subordinate to concerns outside the literary. This school had a lot of resonance at the time, but it aged very poorly. I think that today the majority of *nouveau roman* members have barely any readers. Robbe-Grillet, Nathalie Sarraute, and Claude Simon are very seldomly read, although from an experimental point of view, they did push the novel. There were many discussions surrounding this around the world, and it became a politicized matter.

THE EFFECTS OF TIME ON THE NOVEL

RG: In your opinion, neither Sartre's novels nor the *nouveau roman* have survived the test of time: it would be difficult for them to find readers today. Can you speak about the effects of time on novels? What makes it so that a Sartre novel was so successful in the sixties and has now fallen into oblivion?

MVLL: Books change with the times. With the evolution of daily living, books are viewed from another perspective and can come to change in a very profound way. There are books that at the time seemed funny and ceased being so with the passing of time: *Don Quixote*, for example, was read as a book of humor in its time, but today we read it as a classic, as a very serious work. Although it has humor, today we see in *Don Quixote* a very important testimony—historical, sociological, and anthropological—of the culture of its era. That prevails over the humor that contemporaneous readers appreciated in *Don Quixote*.

Now, the question is: When a book becomes universal, does it lose its specificity? In other words, does it lose local characteristics, the color given to it by virtue of being a book that is very representative of a place, of certain customs, of a certain landscape, of a certain idiosyncrasy? I think that great books can lose some of that specificity with the passing of time, but they also gain something: that's why they manage to keep readers century after century. These books are capable of demonstrating, beyond local color—the picturesque, typical, or folkloric—certain human characteristics with which people of very different cultures can identify. This is what happens to us when we read novels by Faulkner, by Victor

Hugo, by Dostoyevsky, or by Tolstoy. These are works from very diverse cultures, written in different time periods, yet nonetheless today's readers easily identify with the characters because, despite the differences in their customs or in their way of dress, they live experiences that are perfectly understandable to us. In fact, the experiences we find in these novels help us better understand our own reality.

So, what does a novel lose with the passing of time? It loses the specificity of testimony, the local color, the folkloric. But if we're talking about a great novel, it narrates human experiences that are shared by people of very different conditions and cultures, and that is what lends them universality.

What becomes difficult is knowing from the start if a work will stand the test of time. There are authors who write for the readers of their era and think that their work will not survive. But it is very difficult, when you are dealing with works of a certain caliber, to determine which among them will endure. It also depends on the kind of society that will exist in the future. An author who is practically unknown in his own time, such as Kafka, could become extraordinarily relevant with the passing of time because the problems he explored—which in his own time seemed so unrealistic, so unusual—suddenly reflect readers' experiences. Kafka imagined a world of fear, insecurity, panic, terror. Twenty or thirty years after his death, that was the world Europe was experiencing, especially Central and Eastern Europe.

Literature is like a living body that changes according to the context it inhabits. Books that went unnoticed in their time soon gain enormous relevancy because they were ahead of their time and describe experiences that readers would only identify with later, with the evolution of history, the economy, and the culture in general. But if a literary work is not universal, if it cannot be read by readers from other cultures and time periods, that work will come to be an anthropological or sociological document of the period in which it was written.

THE BOOM

RG: We found an example of literature that has stood the test of time in the Boom novels. *Conversation in The Cathedral*, *One Hundred Years of Solitude*, *Hopscotch* all keep finding readers over half a century after their publication. Why have these works of the Boom remained current?

MVLL: Perhaps because the Latin American writers of my generation had a less provincial and more cosmopolitan view. Nearly the entire Boom generation lived abroad. Carpentier spent a good part of his life in France and later in Venezuela, far from Cuba. Carlos Fuentes lived in Mexico but also had a house in London; he spoke different languages and traveled constantly. Cortázar left Argentina in 1951 and from then on lived in France. Borges could be the exception: in his youth, he lived in Switzerland for many years, but then he spent nearly his whole life in Buenos Aires, although he was accused of being a cosmopolitan who evaded national reality. Onetti lived outside of Uruguay, in Buenos Aires. Roa Bastos, the Paraguayan, sought exile in Argentina and in Europe. Donoso studied in the United States, here in Princeton, and was later in Europe. One of the few exceptions was Rulfo, who never left Mexico.

The writers of that generation were very different from one another, but the experience of having lived abroad made them all cosmopolitan. They read writers from other languages, belonging to different movements, and that gave them a universal perspective on literature. Starting with that generation, Latin American literature became less provincial, less localized.

THE BOOM AND THE CUBAN REVOLUTION

RG: The Cuban Revolution was an adrenaline shot for the Boom's writers, as much for those who supported the regime unconditionally as for those who were critical. Never before had there been such an intense relationship between literature and politics in Latin America. What impact did the Cuban Revolution have on your thinking and on your work?

MVLL: My first direct experience with communism occurred in 1953, when I participated in the Communist Party of Peru, a very small organization that didn't even exist as a party anymore because the government had devastated it with so much repression, so many expulsions and imprisonments. The majority of communists were in exile. When I started at the university, I was active in the party for a year, in the Cahuide group, which was the rebuilt Communist Party. There were few of us, but we were very sectarian, dogmatic, completely Stalinist.

I spent that year arguing in my party cell about the relationship between literature and politics. I was a great reader of Sartre and identified with his positions, politics, and aesthetics. Sartre was close to the communists, although he had differences with them: he accepted, for example, historical materialism but not dialectical materialism, and not socialist realism, either. I had many arguments with the party's other members, which was ridiculous because we were so very few, and there were fierce debates about doctrine. I was very critical of the strict dogmatism that reigned in the party, so after a year I separated myself, although I continued being left-wing.

Following that first disappointment, my enthusiasm for militancy was rekindled a few years later by the triumph of the Cuban Revolution. In Peru, I met some exiled Cubans who had been with Fidel in the 26th of July Movement and who had had to flee Batista's dictatorship. One of them worked at the radio with me, and I recall that he gave me a lot of material about the things happening in his country in the 1950s. When the revolution triumphed, I was already living in Europe, but that new wave of hope for Latin America made it all the way there. We thought we were dealing with a revolution that would be neither dogmatic nor intolerant, that would be open, that would allow dissidence and freedom.

The impact of the Cuban Revolution in the world was something extraordinary. It seemed different, like it didn't follow traditional guidelines, because it had been born not from the Communist Party, but from the 26th of July Movement. It was a great novelty that this group of non-communist, anti-imperialist young people achieved the overthrow of a military dictatorship, and practically at the doorstep of the United States. There was, besides, a romantic heroism in the figure of Fidel Castro, in the struggle of the bearded ones in the Sierra Maestra, and all of that seduced people. This model of revolution tried to replicate itself in many countries in Latin America, but it failed all over, except, perhaps, in Nicaragua.

In the early years, almost all Latin American intellectuals were united in the defense of the Cuban Revolution. There were very few exceptions: in Argentina, for example, a group

of writers led by Victoria Ocampo, the founder and editor of
the magazine *Sur*, never wanted to sign any manifestos sup-
porting Cuba. Héctor Murena, an essayist who was very in-
fluential at the time, was another Argentine who maintained
a critical position vis-à-vis the revolution. And Borges, as it
happens, was never interested in Cuba. But apart from them,
there was near unanimity among Latin American writers
who were leftist, centrist, or democratic in sympathizing with
the Cuban Revolution, and although they may not have completely identified with it, they agreed that it was something to
be defended. It represented a new option for Latin America,
because it wasn't a communist revolution, but rather a movement launched by the youth of the 26th of July, who seemed
democratic with a very radical reformist spirit, but democratic nonetheless.

In addition, the Cuban Revolution generated great interest in Latin America, even among writers who had never
been interested. One of these was Cortázar, who had left Argentina very upset; he had broken with his country in order
to organize his whole life in France. This coincided with the
great success of Latin American literature in the 1960s,
something that began to generate a series of relationships between writers from that region who did not previously seek
each other out and who, at times, didn't even know each
other. Suddenly, there was a kind of coming together, of ca-
maraderie, of friendship between those of us living in exile—
voluntarily, as in my case and in that of Cortázar—from our
countries.

Cortázar's case is the most obvious: there was like a redis-
covery of Latin America. Cortázar did not want to return to
Argentina: he had lived in Italy and in France and was very
integrated into that European world, where the literature and

music—jazz—he liked were. When I met him, his lack of interest in politics bordered on disdain: he wasn't interested, and he wouldn't even agree to talk about politics. I recall wanting to introduce him to Luis Goytisolo, who lived in France, but he told me, "I don't want to meet him because he is too political for me." He organized his life around the things he liked, which were literature, music, and painting. And suddenly, he agreed to a trip to Cuba and from that moment on completely changed his way of being. The most extraordinary transformation of a person that I've ever seen took place. He became impassioned over the region and over politics. He became militant and revolutionary. Latin America came to be a central concern of his life, and he began to travel around to different countries. He discovered politics at the age of sixty—in other words, at an age when the majority of people become disillusioned with militancy. Until then, he had created a completely private, personal world for himself, which he greatly protected, because very few people had access to him. And then he changed personalities; he began to live facing outward, practically on the streets. He wanted to rejuvenate himself, and he adopted all of the interests, the positions, the gestures of young people. He discovered eroticism at the same time as the revolution.

During the early sixties, I made many trips to Cuba. The first was in 1962, and I was left dazzled by the mobilization of all Cubans against the threat of a U.S. invasion: it looked like the battle of David against Goliath. I maintained that enthusiastic position until, little by little, I discovered a darker reality. My initial moment of disagreement came when I found out about the UMAP camps, the Military Units to Aid Production, which were concentration camps for homosexuals, common criminals, and counterrevolutionaries established in the provinces. It seemed terrible to me, but I thought that in the vast scheme of things, it was something relatively minor, when compared to all of the benefits the revolution had brought: the military barracks turned into schools; the literacy brigades launched in the sierra to teach peasants how to read and write. It seemed that the revolution had been so generous and so positive, that it had produced such important changes, that such excesses could be forgiven.

My enthusiasm tamped down considerably, and I became more critical. By then, many things had happened in Cuba that we didn't want to see. An example is what happened with *Lunes de Revolución*, a cultural supplement to the newspaper *Revolución*, directed by Guillermo Cabrera Infante since 1959. This was a very high-level literary publication that supported experimentation, with the idea of launching a cultural revolution that would be the counterpart of a political revolution, something that was not allowed in the Soviet Union or in the European socialist countries.

When I traveled to Cuba for the first time in '62, *Lunes de Revolución* had already shut down. The case was a very clear one: it was shut down because it was too free, because it took too many liberties in the cultural field. Little by little, we started realizing that all newspapers and magazines belonged to the state, and when the government exercises a monopoly over information, the press cannot have any other function but that of generating propaganda. But it was very difficult to see that when we were living in the exaltation of those initial times and when what we wanted was to support the revolution and wager on its survival.

All of that generalized enthusiasm came tumbling down with the Padilla affair, which divided the intellectuals of my generation and caused my complete break with the revolution.

There was, on the one hand, a very majoritarian group, fully identified with Cuba. On the other hand was a handful of writers who wanted to maintain an attitude that was critical. We had a lot of mud thrown at us: manifestos against us were published, and there were even some dangerous moments. I recall a theater festival in Manizales, Colombia, that took place shortly after the Padilla affair. There was an event at the university, and when I went up to the podium, besides being on the receiving end of ferocious insults, I was approached by a gentleman who said, "You're not getting out of here alive; if you give me your authorization, I will get your wife out of the auditorium, because you're going to get killed here." It was horrendous. All of us onstage were accused of being imperialists and traitors, although there were invitees who were not. Along with us was, for example, a Spanish theater critic, a militant communist who identified completely with the Cuban Revolution, who, merely for being on that stage, was also vilified.

It was a dangerous atmosphere because of how exacerbated things were. It was a very difficult period because the great majority of writers, intellectuals, and artists identified so much with Cuba that they couldn't see us as anything but CIA agents.

TRANSLATION THEORIES

RG: Now I'd like to talk about another aspect of your novels: the translations. You have worked with some of the most famous translators of the English-speaking world—like Gregory Rabassa and Edith Grossman—and in your correspondence with them, there are debates about the solutions you can provide to a translation problem. Here at Princeton, Jennifer Shyue is researching the correspondence you maintained with Rabassa about the translation of the word *cholo*. Jennifer, can you tell us more?

JENNIFER SHYUE: In a letter dated February 28, 1972, which is in Princeton's archives, Gregory Rabassa explains how he decided to translate *cholo* while preparing the English-language version of *Conversation in The Cathedral*. "The word *cholo*," Rabassa writes, "is difficult and I am opting for a variation, at times highlighting its racial connotation with 'half-breed' and, alternately, the social connotation, with 'peasant.' At times, both can be combined in 'peasant half-breed' or 'half-breed peasant,' if the situation warrants something stronger."

I'm interested in this example because in English, "half-breed" and "peasant" completely change the register of the word *cholo* for a Spanish-speaking reader.

MVLL: "Peasant" doesn't seem like a very good solution to me because *cholo* doesn't mean that. The meaning of that word is very dependent on who says it, to whom it is being said, and the tone with which it is said. *Cholo* can be a term of affection. My mother, for example, would call me "*mi cholito.*" Romantic couples also call each other "*cholita*" and "*cholito.*" Now, when said by a white person, *cholo* can be an insult, a way of reminding someone that he is not white. The original meaning of *cholo* is "mestizo." But there are many interpretations. A very frequent and racist insult is *cholo de mierda*, which is a way of saying, "You're not white, you're an Indian, or practically an Indian." Nevertheless, saying "*cholito*" or "*mi cholito lindo*" or "*mi cholita linda*" turns the word into its opposite and expresses affection, warmth.

Besides, you can always be someone's *cholo*. In the Peru of my childhood, money made people white and poverty made them more *cholo*. A white person who lived in poverty was more *cholo* because *cholos* are associated with society's working classes. It would be very difficult for a wealthy man to be a *cholo*, except among other rich people. Racism was full of subtlety, of complexity. You need to look at the way and the context in which the word *cholo* is used. It's very difficult to translate, to be honest. It doesn't have just one translation in English, but several.

JS: I also found that the translation of the title of *Historia de Mayta* into English generated debate.

MVLL: Yes. I had many debates with the editor and with Alfred Mac Adam, the translator, about the title in English. They didn't like the more literal translation—*The Story of Mayta*—so they named it *The Real Life of Alejandro Mayta*. I was never too happy with that solution. It seemed imprecise to me, and besides, it caused confusion regarding the original.

That title wasn't truthful because the novel doesn't aim to tell "the real story." The main character is a writer trying to write about Mayta's life, but in the end he realizes that the real story eludes him and he ends up drafting a narrative that is rather unreal. He has to invent so much and use his imagination to fill in the details he actually finds. In the end, it comes to be a story that contains more fiction than historical reality. In other words, *The Real Life* is anything but. It would have been more precise to call it *The Invented Life of Alejandro*

Mayta. But they didn't believe me and ended up using that title I have never liked.

JS: Mac Adam writes about that choice: he says it is an ironic title because the novel itself takes apart all notion of reality.

MVLL: That's an a posteriori interpretation, but when a reader sees the book's title, she imagines that what she will find is the real life of Alejandro Mayta. When she reads the novel, she will probably discover that it is ironic, but going in, it is an irony that is not noted at all.

RG: There's another very interesting translation problem that appears in *Who Killed Palomino Molero?* The first word in the novel is *jijunagrandísimas*, which Mac Adam translates as "sons of bitches." Besides changing the register, the game of euphemism and apocope is completely lost.

MVLL: Yes: the local color is lost. In addition, that word is also used to convey very strong emotions. In that case, it's not referring to anyone in particular: saying "*jijunagrandísimas*" is equivalent to exclaiming, "Oh my God! How terrible!" and simply conveys surprise, disgust, stupefaction in the face of the terrible thing being viewed.

RG: Do you get very involved in the translation of your novels?

MVLL: It depends on the translator. If the translator wants me to be involved, I do so with pleasure. But I've always wanted the translator to have complete freedom. I've never believed in the possibility of a literal or absolutely faithful translation.

To me, it seems much more important that a translator be capable of rewriting the work in her own language, taking certain liberties, and that the result be read not as a translation but as an original creation. It is more important that a translator know how to write well in her own language because if she understands the foreign work perfectly but writes poorly, it ruins the translation. In contrast, a writer might not know the work very well and may even make mistakes, but if she writes well in her language, the book that comes out of it will be better. Each language has its own genius, and the important thing is that translation successfully re-create it in such a way that it doesn't sound like a translation. There's nothing worse than reading a book and realizing it's a translation: to feel like something is screeching in the language, that it's false language, that the characters would never speak as they are made to speak in that book. That is why the great translators sometimes take liberties.

A very interesting case is that of Borges, who did marvelous translations from German and English taking very great liberties. Efraín Kristal has studied this case in his book *Invisible Work: Borges and Translation*. When he translated, Borges did things that the authors would have never allowed: if he didn't like the end of a story, he changed it. In other cases, he completely altered the nature of a phrase: if the original sounded off to him, he improved it. His work was very creative, but not something that could be called translation in the strictest sense of the term. The translations are versions that are written in an impeccable Spanish, as Borges's is, but that at times can be read as Borgesian texts and not the writings of the author he translates.

This is also the case with the translation of *If I Forget Thee, Jerusalem*. Faulkner writes in a very particular language, which has a certain cadence, in addition to using very long, complex, and tangled phrases. When Borges translates this novel, the result is a beautiful book, but one that sounds more like Borges than like Faulkner. He has cut phrases to make them short, as he liked them. All of the darkness that characterized Faulkner's prose becomes transparent, clear, translucent, as Borges's prose always is. He takes some liberties that go well beyond what is tolerable, something that doesn't keep his translations from sometimes being better than the original. It's an extreme case.

But faithful translators, the ones who don't want to be creative, also produce very different versions of the original. This is the case with Tolstoy's *War and Peace*. There are at least three translations into Spanish, with many differences between the three. No matter how hard they try to be faithful, the translators ended up inserting something of themselves and can come to recompose the work entirely. What is fundamental is for the translator to work with a certain sense of originality, to take certain liberties in order to find equivalents in her own language.

Because of all of this, if there is a translator who does not want me to bother her, I do not bother her. Almost all translators send me a list of words or expressions that they didn't quite understand, especially very local words or Peruvianisms. I respond and offer explanations. But if they don't ask, I try not to get involved. There are authors who like to oversee things, but I think that, for that, you would need to have a near perfect knowledge not just of the other language but also of the idiosyncrasies behind that language, which a literary work expresses.

2

JOURNALISM AND LITERATURE

Journalism has been one of the central themes in Mario Vargas Llosa's work, from Conversation in The Cathedral *to* A Fish in the Water. *In several of these works, there is a literary version of the journalist's experience that the novelist has accumulated throughout his life, from his time at the daily* La Crónica *at the age of fifteen, to the columns he now writes for* El País. *The relationship between narrative and reporting has been, in addition, a subject of reflection in his articles and essays.*

RUBÉN GALLO: Journalism is an important subject in your work, and in many of your novels there are people who work as reporters at newspapers, radio stations, and other media. In *Conversation in The Cathedral*, the daily *La Crónica* is one of the novel's main spaces: a gray world where young people with literary ideals end up drowning themselves in poverty and alcohol. But in contrast to those characters, you have worked in journalism since you were fifteen years old and you continue to do so with the column you have in *El País*. Can you talk to us about what journalism has represented in your career?

MARIO VARGAS LLOSA: I would like to begin by making a distinction between fiction and journalistic reporting. Many times, journalism relies on literary techniques to relay certain events. There is a school of journalism born in the United States that, although it is rooted in deep investigation, comes very close to literature, because of the type of writing and the organization of the materials. In addition, it uses certain resources taken from fiction, such as suspense or chronological dislocation, to create expectations, curiosity, dramatic tension.

But even in these cases, there is a fundamental difference, and it's that, in principle, journalism should not transgress the truth. It should seek the truth and try to expose it in the most attractive and interesting way possible, but its raison d'être is to present reality as it is. None of that is obligatory in fiction. When one writes fiction, one has the freedom to break with reality, to deeply alter it, while a journalistic report is valued for how closely it aligns with reality. The better the journalistic text expresses reality, the more authentic and genuine it is considered. There is a search for truth that goes beyond the text, and that is what justifies it or takes away its authority. Fiction, in contrast, is valued in and of itself, and its success or failure depends on itself and not on how closely it aligns with reality. A novel can break definitively with reality, expressing another dimension, created by the writer with his imagination and with words, and can sustain itself. In fact, literature always has an added element, something that is not in reality, and that is what is, strictly speaking, literary about fiction.

For me, journalism has been very important because it helped me to discover the reality of my country. In Peru, as in many countries in the Third World, the structure of society is such that the members of one social class know very little about what is happening in other sectors of the population. The Peru where I spent my childhood and adolescence was very limited: I moved in an urban, middle-class world that was Spanish-speaking, Westernized—white, in quotes—and I knew nothing at all about the rest of Peru.

I entered journalism when I was still a student—it was the vacation break between fifth and sixth form, between the second-to-last and the last year of school. I was fifteen years old, and I came in as a reporter at a newspaper that sent me to cover all kinds of things in a city I knew only partially. I had never been in the poor neighborhoods, in the marginal areas, the places that had the highest number of outbreaks of violence. I worked for a few weeks on the police beat, which reported on Lima's poorest and most violent parts. Thus I went discovering a country with which I was completely unfamiliar. In that sense, the experience of journalism was very instructive: it taught me so much about the reality of a country that was more complex, much more turbulent, much more violent than the one I had lived in until then.

There is another interesting aspect: I thought that journalism was close to literature and that I could live off that activity while I kept writing. But a journalist's use of language and a writer's use are completely different. The most professional journalism is one that prizes reality above form: the more neutral and transparent the language, the more efficient it ends up being from a journalistic point of view. The use of language a writer makes is the complete opposite: its duty is to affirm a personal vision, to express the writer's individuality through words, and to do so with a certain originality, in other words, with a certain distance from common and standard language. That is what literature does, as we can see if we read Rulfo, García Márquez, Onetti, and analyze the types of language those writers use.

A journalist does not have the luxury of being original when it comes to writing: he is forced to leave aside his personality, to dissolve it within that functional language belonging to dailies. It is true that there are many writers who have also been journalists, but I think that when it comes to writing a novel, when it comes to making literature, they use a language that is very different from the one they employ while drafting a news story, a chronicle, or an editorial. This is the first incompatibility that exists between journalism and literature.

That said, the role of journalism within a democratic society is very important. I grew up in Peru, during a period of dictatorship—remember that General Odría's dictatorship lasted from 1948 to 1956—and those years were fundamental for my generation. We were boys still when General Odría led a coup, and we were men when he left power and democracy came. All of our childhood and adolescence was lived in a world where there was very strict censorship: we knew that the press lied, that instead of describing reality, it hid it and manipulated it. It was a servile press that praised power and that was in the service of the dictatorship. Journalism was one of the main instruments the government had to manipulate reality, to make us believe we lived in a perfect world. Journalism is a fundamental barometer of the degree of freedom that exists in a society: we need that right to criticize, that right of expression that leads to true journalism so that a society can be fully democratic.

In the modern era, journalism has suffered another distortion, very unlike censorship, and that is frivolization. This is a very contemporary phenomenon: the frivolous press has always existed, but before, it was a marginal practice. Today, that frivolization has made its way to the great papers, even the bodies that we consider to be the most serious, for a very practical reason: a magazine, a newspaper, or a TV program that tries to be exclusively serious ends up being a failure from an economic point of view. There is constant pressure on the media to conquer great masses of readers or viewers.

I lived in England for many years, and I recall that when I arrived, in 1966, journalism was of a nearly funeral-like seriousness. At that time, *The Times* had great style: sober language and a vocation for objectivity. I could have never imagined that *The Times* and the *Daily Mail* would end up resembling each other: the dosage of frivolity present now would have been inconceivable for what *The Times* was twenty or thirty years ago. That banality has been filtering into the press of our time. I think it is a change that reflects the deterioration of culture in the world, something that has deeply wounded the basis of democratic societies.

RG: We see that change in the expanse of articles. Twenty years ago, a newspaper like *The New York Times* or *The Guardian* used to publish articles that were 5,000, 7,500, 10,000 words long, something that now seems unthinkable. Although brevity is not incompatible with seriousness: your articles in *El País* are limited to 1,250 words and in that space, you manage to develop serious ideas and relate them to political events and even literary works. The limit of 1,250 words can also be seen as a literary exercise: let's recall that many writers, from Augusto Monterroso to Jorge Luis Borges, have always given a privileged position to brief formats.

MVLL: Articles are a genre. Great article writers are capable of developing a single idea. A well-achieved article has one central idea: from there flows the reasoning for the rest of the piece, just like complementary ideas prepare the reader and later soothe him if he has been left too shocked. We can see it in the work of that great U.S. journalist Walter Lippmann, who was an extraordinary writer of articles, capable of developing an entire thought in 750 or 1,000 words. His articles always present an idea that is the backbone around which the rest of the text is structured.

Articles are a difficult genre, but they can also be a space for a lot of creativity. I remember that when I got to England in 1966, I impatiently awaited Sundays so I could read articles by two critics: Cyril Connolly, the author of *Enemies of Promise*, wrote a weekly literary chronicle in *The Sunday Times* commenting on some book or some literary event, and his observations were always dazzling. He had that extraordinary capacity for developing a whole thought in an article of 750 or 1,000 words. And there was another critic, Kenneth Tynan, who was more frivolous and more playful, who critiqued theater and was also absolutely extraordinary because he succeeded in getting the reader to visualize the show on which he was commenting. And he did so with great elegance, with great humor. Afterward, he himself came to write a play, *Oh! Calcutta!*, that was successful the world over. He became rich and stopped writing articles. Incidentally, the title of his work was a word game: *Oh, quel cul t'as.*

These two article-writers were also great creators. They cultivated a genre that was considered a minor one, but in it they managed to be deeply creative.

JOURNALISM AND THE BOHEMIAN LIFE

RG: In several of your books—from *Conversation in The Cathedral* to *A Fish in the Water*—journalism appears as a trap for the writer. Among the characters, we see talented young people who could have been writers but who, upon beginning to work as journalists, lose themselves and end up trapped. They don't manage to leave the newsroom and never publish the great novel they would have wanted to write.

MVLL: So it is. Because the world of journalism that I knew was very marked by bohemian nightlife. Writing was done at night, and the night was sinful and tempting. Journalists finished their shift, went out for some drinks, and stayed out until dawn. That lifestyle ended up killing all the energy and discipline that are fundamental to a creator. At one time, it was thought that the bohemian life was a good laboratory for literature, but that's a romantic fantasy because all great writers have been hard workers and disciplined, and have organized their lives around writing. There are a few cases of great creators who lived a bohemian nightlife and, although they quickly burnt out, left some work behind, but I think that's the exception rather than the rule.

When I began working as a journalist, I met many colleagues who would have liked to have been writers and who lived with a great nostalgia for the poetry they never wrote, for the novels they never published, because their lives became trapped in the routine of journalism, in work that is not only anonymous but also ephemeral. News lasts twenty-four hours—sometimes less—and then newspapers are thrown in the trash. That fleeting nature of journalism really frustrated the writers, who always longed for achieving transcendence.

THE PRACTICE OF JOURNALISM

RG: You've practiced journalism throughout your life, and now you continue to write a column for *El País*. Why have you decided to keep writing articles instead of devoting all of your time to literature?

MVLL: I've never wanted to abandon journalism for one very clear reason: although literature is my vocation—it's the most stimulating job in the world—I have never admired the figure of the writer who is just a writer, who lives completely shut away with his ghosts, in a mental world that distances him from daily reality, from the day-to-day life, from the experience that is the common denominator among people. Perhaps because I am a realist writer and not a fantasy writer, I never try to create a world that is completely sovereign, independent of the real world. In my novels, I have wanted to show a world that has at least the appearance of the real world. That's why the idea of performing a job that can lead me to divorce myself completely from that world doesn't tempt me. For me, journalism has been a way to always keep a foot in the real world, and that's why I keep practicing it. It's my way of not separating myself from that objective, shared, daily reality. My articles deal with literary themes, but also with social or political events relating to daily life. The foot in reality that journalism gives me is very important for my work. I recall one of Vallejos's verses that goes, "to eat something pleasant and go out / in the afternoon, to buy a good newspaper."

Reading a good newspaper is a very stimulating experience, almost as much as reading a good book, because a well-written article puts us in touch with what is happening and makes us feel part of that diverse, complex phenomenon that is the here and now. That type of serious journalism has been getting lost little by little in our era and replaced by something more basic, made of headlines. It would seem that the great articles have become impossible for newspapers because there are no readers for them.

RG: Your articles deal with a great variety of subjects. You have written about Fidel Castro, about Margaret Thatcher, about the pope and his pronouncements against condoms, about the only student you had at Cambridge, about Latin America's tendencies toward populism, about Donald Trump, about the war in Iraq and elections in Argentina. Besides erudition and versatility, this list of subjects demonstrates a great intellectual freedom, a curiosity that leads you to interrogate very different aspects of the world in which we live.

MVLL: I greatly appreciate that freedom. I'm forced to turn in an article every two weeks, but the subject is open. It's marvelous to be able to write about whatever I find most stimulating. I always write about current subjects because I feel that is the role of journalism. Besides, I like to do so because a large part of the time, I live behind the times, writing novels, separated from the here and now.

LARA NORGAARD: Let's stay on the subject of journalism: the edition of your *Complete Works* includes only the articles you wrote after 1968. What changed in your journalistic work that year, and why did you decide to start with that date? Why didn't you include the articles you wrote when you were younger?

MVLL: I wasn't in charge of the selection—that was entrusted to Antoni Munné, the collection's director at Galaxia Gutenberg. I gave him carte blanche because he is very familiar with my work and has respectable criteria. It's true that a collection of complete works, if it does as the title says, should include everything: the good and the bad. Perhaps I would have included many bad articles, but he preferred to eliminate the ones I wrote when I was very young because they seemed to him to be the least interesting and the least relevant.

I think if those articles show anything, it's how much I've changed in my way of thinking, especially regarding politics. In collections of articles or essays, I've been careful about including articles that are contradictory to demonstrate that there has been a change and an evolution.

RG: That shows that complete works are never actually complete. Once they've been published, another text could always show up, another letter, a version that was left out of what was supposed to be the definitive edition. Augusto Monterroso mocked this concept, which, when you really think about it, is nearly metaphysical, in a little book of stories bearing the title *Complete Works*.

MVLL: Yes, of course: *Complete Works and Other Stories*. That book also contains "Dinosaur," the shortest and most perfect story ever written and that consists of only one sentence:

"When he awoke, the dinosaur was still there." These eight words contain an entire story, with great economy. It is the opposite of *Complete Works* because it is incomplete, but what's missing is what makes it a great story.

LN: When you speak of changes in your articles, would you say that they are mainly political changes?

MVLL: Political, but also literary. As a young man, I admired Sartre enormously, to such a degree that my friends mocked me and gave me the nickname "Brave Little Sartre." I wouldn't be able to read Sartre today: I realize that those novels I found so exciting as a young man are bad and, at the end of the day, not very interesting. Now I would say that Sartre was imitating Dos Passos, but Dos Passos really did have a great talent for novels and Sartre didn't: he was too intelligent to be a great novelist. To write, you can't let yourself be guided by ideas: you have to hand yourself over to emotions and passions, something that Sartre was never able to do because he was a thinking machine, a robot. He was enormously intelligent, which works for writing good essays, but not for creating good novels.

RG: Sartre lacked body.

MVLL: He lacked body, he lacked sweat, he lacked tears, he lacked love, he lacked passion. But he didn't want any of that. He was a thinking machine and that is why his novels seem like essays: they're reiterations of ideas, novel-like threads of debates, but without any of the literary elements that make a good novel.

JOURNALISM AND CENSORSHIP

LN: On the subject of censorship of the press: in Peru, under Odría, censorship was practiced not only by the owners of newspapers but also by reporters themselves because they predicted what wouldn't get through. It was a type of self-censorship that ended up being more important and nefarious than official censorship.

MVLL: When I worked at *La Crónica*, there were words that could not be used and subjects that could not be mentioned. It was an automatic thing. You came to develop a sort of second nature as a person who was perfectly aware of the dangerous terrain you could not enter unless you wanted to run a risk. And that's why there was clandestine journalism, to which the little newspaper from our group Cahuide belonged. But this self-censorship didn't just affect journalism: it also determined civic behavior, because there were things you couldn't do without taking a risk. It's a phenomenon that is typical of all dictatorships, whether they be right-wing or left-wing, ideological or military, religious or lay. A kind of secret personality is immediately created to be ever vigilant, telling the person, "No, not this way. Not this. It's best to avoid this. You shouldn't do this. This implies a risk." That self-censorship is the worst thing that can exist in a society, because it has to do with a censor you carry inside.

LN: Did this kind of self-censorship also arise in other Latin American countries?

MVLL: At the time at which censorship is established, self-censorship comes about immediately, it is always one of the most perverse effects of a dictatorship. I lived it myself in Peru, as a young man, and also in Spain: when I arrived in Madrid in 1958, during Franco's rule, there was prior censorship that required authors and editors to receive approval before publishing. That led many writers to self-censorship because they knew they were going to have things cut from what they had written, so they created an almost automatic mechanism when they wrote, as if they had a little censor inside their heads telling them what not to explore. In another, more subtle and complex sense, self-censorship can have the opposite effect and lead writers to touch on exactly that which is forbidden, to write in defiance of prohibitions. This also corrupts, because if a writer writes only in response to censorship, he loses his freedom. Freedom is a fundamental space when it comes to writing, when it comes to thinking, when it comes to fantasizing. Censorship is an element that distorts in many senses.

Censorship can also be haphazard. Juan Marsé says that when one of his novels went through the censors, they eliminated every instance of the word "armpit." It was absolutely incomprehensible—why "armpit" and not another word? Perhaps because the censor was a pervert and the word "armpit" inspired all manner of salacious images for him. There is no other explanation: the word "armpit" doesn't harm anyone.

When I published my first novel, *The Time of the Hero*, I had an argument with the head censor. At the time, Franco had appointed a group of supposedly progressive ministers— at least in comparison to the previous ones, who had been completely caveman-like. Carlos Robles Piquer, who was the head of information and in charge of censorship, agreed to discuss the changes he proposed to my book with me. So we met for lunch and it was very funny, because one of the sentences he wanted to change was the description of the director of a military school. I had written that the colonel "had a belly like a cetacean," in other words, that he had a big belly. But Robles Piquer said that since the colonel was the director of the barracks, if I mocked him, I was ridiculing not just a person but rather an entire institution, because he represented the army. He explained that if the character were one rank lower, if he were a commander or a captain, then it wouldn't matter as much, but a colonel was a key position in the hierarchy. To egg him on, it occurred to me to ask, "And what happens if instead of saying 'the belly of a cetacean,' I say 'the belly of a whale'?" And he said that the word "whale" could go through, because it seemed less harsh. There we see that censorship is, among other things, a form of stupidity because it wastes so much time on this type of foolishness.

Another sentence he wanted to change was the description of a priest that said: "He has been seen wandering about the brothels of Callao with covetous eyes." And Mr. Robles Piquer said to me, "Look, I know there are clergy who sin, but in your novel, this one is the only priest. If there were another one, you would see that there are good ones and bad ones, but here, we only see the bad one." So I said to him, "Well, what happens if instead of 'brothels,' we put 'houses of prostitution'?" And he said yes, that the phrase "houses of prostitution" could go because it was less harsh. In the end, they changed eight words of mine in the novel's first edition, but Carlos Barral, my editor, was very courageous and restored those eight words to the second edition and nothing happened.

RG: The work of censorship requires a relatively close reading of the text.

MVLL: It is a very detailed reading, but they always have to find something to censor. They're looking for sin, a short-coming, dissidence, and if it doesn't show up, then it has to be invented. Besides, the censor pours his own personal phobias and prejudices into the books he reads. I don't know how there hasn't been a tell-all book about censorship published in Spain, relaying all these cases.

Another example: The film critic Román Gubern wrote a study about King Kong in the movies and proposed the title *Beauty and the Beast*. The censors forbade the title: they said the book could be published as long as the name was changed. He went to talk to someone and said he didn't understand what could be bad about a title like *Beauty and the Beast*. Then the censor said something marvelous: "Look, we're not stupid. What does the title mean? Who is Beauty? Well, obviously, it's Spain. And who's the Beast? We already know you're referring to Generalissimo Franco, so it can't go through." The censor's mental perversion can reach those grotesque extremes: a book about King Kong that is seen as an insult to Franco.

LN: Did that same careful reading process for newspaper articles exist?

MVLL: It was even greater. Censorship increased with the popularity of the genre; that's why the area of most freedom was poetry, because it was thought that very few people read poetry. Poets could express themselves about subjects that were inconceivable in a novel. Censorship was much stricter in novels, more so with newspapers, but where it was truly ferocious was in television. When I got to Spain as a student in 1958, Analía Gadé, an actress who was very famous at the time, told me how censorship worked in television. Before going on air, the censor took out a measuring tape and measured the actresses' skirts and décolleté and would suddenly say, "They have to be longer so that they show less leg," and "The décolleté has to be covered up more so we see less of her chest." That was extremely humiliating for the poor actresses. I imagine that situation must generate all kinds of perversion among the censors.

RG: Have your books been censored in other countries?

MVLL: My books were banned in Cuba after I started to criticize the Cuban government. This is what happens in dictatorships, whose objective is to control literature, art, and creativity, because they consider independent thought to be dangerous. In a democracy, no one believes that a novel or a poem can be dangerous or subversive. I would say in this case, democracies are mistaken and dictatorships have it right, because literature *is* dangerous. Literature teaches us to look at the world with a critical eye. When we read a great novel—*Moby-Dick, Les Misérables, War and Peace, Don Quixote*—and then we return to the real world, something has changed within us that makes us more critical of what we see around us. Reading a good novel means inhabiting a perfect world, round and polished, characterized by beauty, where even evil becomes something attractive. Everything takes place in a literary language that allows us to reach a deep understanding of everything that is happening, its causes and effects. In comparison to literature, the real world is imperfect, unorganized, chaotic. So reading a good novel makes us very critical of everything around us, and this is extremely subversive in a society that seeks to exercise complete control over the individual. That explains the mistrust dictators feel toward literature . . . and they're right.

In a controlled society, people read in a different way and try to find in books, in novels, in stories, in plays, something that isn't found in newspapers, or on television, or on the radio: a critical analysis of what is happening. Literature becomes a means for expressing reflections on the world and acquires a political importance that it does not have in democracies. Poetry, novels, literary essays, and theater become full of allusions that people immediately interpret as a function of the experience they are living through. Then literature becomes something much more important: it acquires political importance. People who live under a dictatorship seek in books the false bottom that speaks of a reality that has been rigorously suppressed in the official media. That is why dictatorships are so concerned with what writers do. Literature is something that undermines the certainty that the dictatorship wants to impose on society.

For writers, it ends up being very stimulating to rely on the thousand and one ways literature has of saying things without doing so explicitly in order to mock the censors.

RG: Many writers create their work against dictatorships. I am thinking of Milan Kundera, who wrote marvelous works, such as *The Unbearable Lightness of Being*, during the hardest era of Czech socialism. With the fall of the socialist bloc in the early nineties, the air is let out of Kundera as a writer. Everything he publishes after no longer has that form, that hate, that rage it had when he was fighting against the great enemy that was the socialist state, which threatened him with jail, with very harsh sentences.

We see a similar phenomenon in Carlos Saura: the films

he made under Franco—such as *Cría cuervos* (Raise ravens)—
are charged with political commentary, but after Franco's
death, he devoted himself to doing full-length films about
flamenco, tango, and other subjects that have nothing to do
with politics.

MVLL: This phenomenon arises in all dictatorships: one writes
against the dictatorship, and when the dictatorship falls, suddenly, the enemy that allowed one to think and work is lost.
Another example would be the German expressionist art that
arose between the First and Second World Wars. Germany
was completely upside down, with very violent conflicts in
those years: communists and Nazis were killing each other on
the streets. But that unsafe and precarious life was responsible
for the emergence of an enormously creative art of shocking
violence. Among the artists of those years, there is one whom
I admire very much: George Grosz, one of the most ferocious
critics of Nazism and of racism, who was saved by a miracle.
A Nazi commando unit went to his house, looking for him.
He received them but acted like the butler: he had them
enter, he offered them tea, while the Nazis were drinking tea,
he escaped by a small staircase and went all the way to the
United States. But as soon as he stepped on the American
continent, all of his ferocity, his bellicosity, disappeared, all
of the atrocious caricatures that had characterized his work.
One would say he became good, that he lost his animosity: he
began to create paintings that were completely decorative,
sane, benign, without any force or soul. He never again
recovered the energy he'd had in Germany. He needed to hate
in order to be a great painter. When he stopped hating and
started living in a country where he hated no one, and where
he felt very happy, his painting lost its soul completely. It's a

very interesting case. There are many other cases of writers who needed to have a fearful adversary in order to create.

BEN HUMMEL: Heberto Padilla?

MVLL: Yes, exactly, that's also the case of Heberto Padilla. Let's recall the facts: Padilla was a very good Cuban poet, who in addition had a lot of bitterness. He suffered through a terrible experience: the Cuban authorities accused him of being a dissident and put him in jail. He came out of prison to perform a terrible self-criticism, accusing himself of being a CIA agent and other idiocies, obviously out of fear. Nothing else happened to him, and he stayed in Cuba until finally, many years later, he sought exile in the United States. But the person who arrived in Miami was like the walking dead: he could no longer write anything truly important. The poetry he published was extremely impoverished, as if he had lost his soul. It is a case very similar to that of Grosz. So Padilla lived the rest of his days like a ghost of himself. Perhaps that is why they let him leave, because he could no longer hurt anyone with what he was writing, the saddest thing that can be said about a writer.

3

CONVERSATION IN THE CATHEDRAL

Conversation in The Cathedral (1969) is one of Mario Vargas Llosa's most ambitious books and perhaps the best example of how the writer uses literature to think through the political. Set during Manuel Odría's dictatorship (1948–1956), the novel narrates the moral downfall of Santiago Zavala, a middle-class youth whose high intellectual and literary ambitions are flattened by the dictatorship's power to corrupt. It penetrates all of the city's spaces and all levels of society.

STRUCTURE AND LITERARY TECHNIQUES

RUBÉN GALLO: I'd like to analyze the literary techniques that appear in *Conversation in The Cathedral*. The novel requires great effort on the part of the reader to follow the jumps in time, the changes in point of view, the flashbacks. In that sense, it can be categorized as "difficult literature" that challenges the reader and asks for an investment of time, concentration, and participation to decipher the literary symbols. The novel was published in 1969, during a period of great debate about novelistic techniques in which the options ranged from socialist realism to the *nouveau roman*. What did it mean at the time to bet on difficult literature that requires a considerable investment on the part of the reader in terms of time, mental energy, concentration?

MARIO VARGAS LLOSA: I would like to relay how I arrived at the structure of *Conversation*. I wanted to write a novel about the dictatorship that could show the effects that Odría's regime had on society as a whole, in other words, among Peruvians of different social classes. I spent my adolescence living under the dictatorship, and it wasn't until 1956, when I was twenty years old, that we had free elections. I began to write this novel well after: in the 1960s already, when I was living outside Peru. I started writing unconnected episodes, with different characters—a bodyguard, a maid, a successful businessman, a middle-class kid—and working, in addition, with great confusion, because at the time, I didn't know what order I would impose on all of that. I thought a lot about and considered many options, until I had the idea that the backbone of the story would be a conversation, but a conversation that would have interruptions because other conversations would come in and out.

That is the structure of *Conversation in The Cathedral*: a conversation between Zavalita and Ambrosio, the bodyguard who was his father's chauffeur and lover. This conversation occurs after Zavalita goes to rescue his dog from the municipal dog pound and runs into Ambrosio, who has hit rock bottom and works as a dogcatcher. The two go to have a beer at that little bar near the dog pound called The Cathedral. That's the axis of the story: a conversation that appears and later disappears for long periods but that always reappears. That backbone unites other stories that are scattered over space and time, and that jump from one character to another. One character who comes up in the conversation between Zavalita and Ambrosio can summon another character and evoke a story they both lived in the past, to later return to the main story, summon another character, and on and on.

The main conversation between Zavalita and Ambrosio is like a sort of trunk from which several branches emerge, and those branches end up drawing the tree that is the full story. It didn't matter to me that that could confuse the reader. On the contrary, I thought that confusion was necessary to make the story credible. If the story had been clear from the start, it wouldn't be accepted by the reader. There was too much gruesomeness, too many excesses in everything that happened, and it was best for that story to come out in an opaque way so that the reader herself, led by curiosity and the desire to know, would creatively contribute to piecing together the plot.

I wanted the story to take shape in the reader's memory as she put each figure in its place, as if it were a great puzzle. Of all the novels I have written, *Conversation in The Cathedral* is probably the one that took me the most work. I wrote it just after *The Green House*, which was a novel very influenced by Faulkner, in which the language stands between the reader and the story as if it were a very imposing character. I didn't want the same thing to happen in *Conversation in The Cathedral*, and perhaps that is why the language tries to be transparent, purely functional, to the point that the story seems to have a life of its own, without going through language. I sought to use completely invisible language. I worked a lot on the different drafts of the novel, eliminating all use of language that wasn't a pure instrument of the plot. Those first versions of *Conversation in The Cathedral*, which are much broader than the published novel, are in the archives of Princeton's library. Then I trimmed and trimmed, cutting a lot, looking for that purity of language that neither *The Green House* nor *The Time of the Hero* had.

That structure had an additional advantage: if I had developed the whole story chronologically, I would have had to write not just a book but a saga, because it's a story that contains many different plots, which can be read as stand-alone stories. But the structure of the main conversation allowed me to tell the essential part of each story, to work with hidden details and to obscure a good part of the history and the consequences of certain anecdotes that the reader could imagine for herself to round out the plots bit by bit.

I've been asked a lot about the form of *Conversation in The Cathedral*, and I think the form is fundamental because literature is form: it's structure and how time is organized. But I've never been interested in the disassociated form of the story, of the characters, of the plot. My starting point in writing a novel has always been a story, a character, or a given situation. Then the form starts taking shape, which allows me to clearly see what wants to be told. The difficult work of creativity consists of finding the form that best allows use of the anecdote to make the characters and events narrated stand out and be more believable. The form transpires from the anecdote itself and, at the same time, allows me to see clearly, because I never see clearly until I have the story done.

The way I work crystallized when I wrote *Conversation in The Cathedral*. When I began to write, I felt lost in great confusion, with very vague notions about form, until I had the idea of that main conversation that summoned other conversations.

RG: In 1992, *Vuelta* magazine published an issue devoted to "the defense of difficult literature" in which you also participated. At the time, there was political pressure to make a kind of literature that would be accessible to a wide audience, but you, like many writers, defended that kind of difficult literature.

MVLL: The difficulty comes not from a purely artistic will, but rather from a need to represent a complicated reality, a complicated life, a complicated world. Chivalric novels, for example, present a reality that has only two dimensions: they relay what is lived, and their experience is ignorant of a good deal of reality. But the novel evolves along with history and the advances of civilization. In the modern world, we know there is a dimension to our personalities that we don't control but that is there and that in some way guides our behavior: there is a fascinating inner life. The modern novel wants to come to express all of the dimensions of that reality. But what can you do to express that secret dimension of inner life? You have to find a language and a structure capable of communicating it. What Joyce does is not gratuitous: he invents a language, a form, to express the world that arises from the subconscious, a dimension that does not go through reason. He created a form that in some way introduces the reader to that interiority. To write a novel after Joyce, after Faulkner, is no longer the same: it's no longer possible to write with the naïveté of a nineteenth-century novelist. We can admire nineteenth-century literature, but today, no one would be able to write like Stendhal because that form expresses just a fragment of our twenty-first-century reality. The complexity of the novel is born of the confrontation with a world that is infinitely richer, more diverse, subtler than the one our ancestors knew. Great modern writers have been capable, within the tradition, of creating new techniques and new structures that allow the telling of those new levels of reality that make up the knowledge of our time.

RG: Could you speak to us about the authors you read while you were writing the novel?

MVLL: There are several authors whom I read and who left their mark on *Conversation in The Cathedral*: Faulkner, but also Dos Passos, who taught me how to describe the modern city. *USA*, Dos Passos's trilogy, is one of the great modern novels: it uses a novel technique to show a city in motion, with dozens and dozens of characters who show the social complexity of the ant farm that is the modern metropolis and the effervescence that marks the rhythm of our time. In the case of this writer, the complexity comes from the desire to create literature that expresses the reality of the modern world.

RG: Let's look at a concrete example of narrative technique that appears in *Conversation*. In the second chapter of the first book, there is a scene in which Zavalita and Popeye try to seduce the maid Amalia. There's a dialogue between the two friends that is later layered with another dialogue they maintain from months later in another place. The first conversation occurs at the Zavala home, when the two friends and the maid are discovered in the bedroom by Zavalita's parents, who return home unexpectedly. In that scene, there's another interwoven dialogue between the same characters—Zavalita, Popeye, and Amalia—that occurs weeks later at Amalia's house, when the two young men go visit her to take her five pounds because they feel guilty about what happened. In this scene, the temporal and spatial jumps are very clear:

"Your mother had forgotten that she'd invited people to lunch tomorrow," Don Fermín said. "Your mother's out-bursts, otherwise . . ."

Out of the corner of his eye, Popeye saw Amalia go out with the tray in her hands, she was looking at the floor and walking straight, they were in luck.

"Your sister stayed at the Vallarinos'," Don Fermín said. "All in all, my plans for a rest this weekend didn't work out."

"Is it twelve o'clock already, ma'am?" Popeye asked. "I've got to run. We didn't pay any attention to the time, I thought it must have been ten."

"How are things with the senator?" Don Fermín asked. "We haven't seen him at the club in ages."

She went to the street with them and there Santiago patted her on the shoulder and Popeye said good-bye: *ciao*, Amalia. They went off in the direction of the streetcar line. They went into El Triunfo to buy some cigarettes; it was already boiling over with drinkers and pool players.

"A hundred soles for nothing, a wild bit of showing off," Popeye said. "It turned out that we did the girl a favor, now your old man has got her a better job."

"Even so, we got her in a jam," Santiago said. "I'm not sorry about those hundred soles."

"I don't want to keep harping on it, but you're broke," Popeye said. "What did we do to her? Now that you've given her five pounds, forget about your remorse."

Following the streetcar line, they went down to Ricardo Palma and they walked along smoking under the trees on the boulevard between rows of cars.

"Didn't it make you laugh when she talked about Coca-Cola that way?" Popeye laughed. "Do you think she's that dumb or was she putting on? I don't know how I held back, I was pissing inside wanting to laugh."

"I'm going to ask you something," Santiago says. "Do I have the face of a son of a bitch?"

"And I'm going to tell you something," Popeye said. "Don't you think her going out to buy the Coca-Cola for us was strictly hypocritical? As if she was letting herself go to see if we'd repeat what happened the other night."

"You've got a rotten mind, Freckle Face," Santiago said.

"What a question," Ambrosio says. "Of course not, boy."

"O.K., so the breed girl is a saint and I've got a rotten mind," Popeye said. "Let's go to your house and listen to records, then."

"You did it for me?" Don Fermín asked. "For me, you poor black crazy son of a bitch?"

"I swear you don't, son." Ambrosio laughs. "Are you making fun of me?"

"Teté isn't home," Santiago said. "She went to an early show with some girl friends."

"Listen, don't be a son of a bitch, Skinny," Popeye said. "You're lying, aren't you? You promised, Skinny."

"You mean that sons of bitches don't have the faces of sons of bitches, Ambrosio," Santiago says.

MVLL: It's a very well-chosen passage, because you can see different times and episodes here. There is a main conversation, what I call the novel's backbone, the conversation between Ambrosio and Zavalita: we're there when Santiago says, "I'm going to ask you something," we know because of the verbal tense of the narration, which is in the present. Every time the present shows up, we again see certain moments in the conversation between Ambrosio and Zavalita, because it is not all literally reproduced: there are only certain key fragments, which are summoned by the context, by another anecdote that is being told and that alludes in some way to that moment of dialogue between Ambrosio and Zavalita.

When Santiago asks Ambrosio, "Do I have the face of a son of a bitch?" many dialogues from other stories follow until the response suddenly appears. "'I swear you don't, son,' Ambrosio laughs. 'Are you making fun of me?'" And with that, we return to the main conversation, in which Zavalita's comment is placed: "You mean that sons of bitches don't have the faces of sons of bitches, Ambrosio," Santiago says.

There is another conversation interwoven there, between Ambrosio and his employer, Don Fermín. We don't know where or when it occurs, but we know that it appears, interspersed there: "'You did it for me?' Don Fermín asked. 'For me, you poor black crazy son of a bitch?'" What did Ambrosio do for Don Fermín? It's an allusion to the crime that Ambrosio, the Black man, did out of loyalty, out of respect, out of love for his employer and that the reader will later discover. But it's the only allusion to that crime in this section.

We have two very different situations and time periods here, although with characters in common: Ambrosio participates in both conversations. There is another conversation that pops up there, between Popeye and Santiago, that also occurs in two different time periods. Popeye and Zavalita have gone to see Amalia—the reader knows that the Zavalas kicked her out of the house after finding her in bed with

Zavalita and Popeye—because Zavalita feels regret and convinces his friend to go to the *chola*'s house to take five pounds to her. Then there are allusions to the episode in which that happened, that are interwoven with the conversation Popeye and Zavalita maintain after having given the money to Amalia. There's yet another episode: the moment in which Don Fermín and the mother arrive at the house and discover Popeye and Santiago trying to rape the maid.

If those episodes had been told separately, with the corresponding chronological order, that two-page dialogue would have required twenty or thirty pages. Time here is an artificial construction of realistic events. There is nothing that is not believable: everything is perfectly recognizable through the reader's own experience. The only thing that is not realistic is the structure, the way time is organized. That's very important because every novel creates its own time, which can sometimes seem like real time, although it is never real time because there are silences and details that have been hidden. A novel that sought to narrate it all would cause infinite vertigo.

Claude Simon, one of the novelists of the *nouveau roman*, wrote an essay to show that realism is impossible. The essay stated: If realism exists, let's do an exercise in which we describe a pack of Gauloise cigarettes in a realistic way, including all possible details about that object. We'll begin, Simon writes, by describing the box: its size and its design. Then we'll describe what the box contains: the Gauloise cigarettes, the paper they are made of, as well as the tobacco. But we can't stop there; if we did, we wouldn't be realists. We'd have to go to the source and ask, What is the origin of that tobacco? And specify whether we're dealing with tobacco from Cuba, from Santo Domingo, from Martinique. What about the paper? Where are the factories that manufacture that paper? And let's not forget about the distribution system that moves all of those ingredients.

The description of that pack of cigarettes ends up being impossible, because to be truly realistic, the writer could spend his whole life making an inventory of all the elements making up that pack of cigarettes. That is why Claude Simon concludes that realism doesn't exist and the most a writer who believes himself to be a realist can do is synthesize and create narrative apocopes of a reality that is infinite and that is marked by a dizzying number of variables. Literature is never realist, although it may seem so, because it is always dependent on the personality of the writer, on his or her ability to synthesize, to fantasize, and on his or her interests. Claude Simon's thesis is useful in thinking about *Conversation in The Cathedral*: the events narrated there are realistic—there is nothing magical or supernatural in the plot—but time, and the way those different times come together despite their occurring at different times in the experiences of the characters, makes that construction literary and not realist.

RG: It would seem that *Conversation in The Cathedral* sets a trap for the reader: the same characters appear—in this case, Popeye, Zavalita, Amalia—and we follow their dialogue along, but suddenly, there's a jump in space that takes us, without warning, from Zavala's house onto the street. Those types of jumps cause the reader to become disoriented and leave her unsure of whether she is in the same temporal space or whether there has been a change.

MVLL: There are many jumps in time in the novel, but what matters is that the plot always maintains a certain unity, which in this case is provided by the characters, who are in both stories: the one inside the Zavala house and the one on the street. The characters make a link, are the common denominator in those two episodes, which are united in the narration and occur in two different times and spaces. It can be confusing in an initial reading, of course, but the reader's memory reconstructs the chronology and weaves it into the plot, perhaps not always very precisely, but this doesn't affect the story's broader sense.

It is true that this technique makes for difficult reading, because it demands the reader's participation. It is not for passive readers but for very attentive ones, capable of constantly reconstructing a dismembered reality. But that dismemberment is not artificial, because if it were told another way, the story would end up being too gruesome, too banal, too predictable. The mystery, the density, the intensity of the plot of *Conversation in The Cathedral* comes precisely from its structure and its narrative technique.

RG: What order did you follow during the process of writing the novel? Did you first write some stories and then others? First the story at the Zavala house and then the visit to Amalia's house?

MVLL: I wrote episodes here and there first, until I found the structure, with the main conversation and other conversations coming in and out, like calls, because of allusions, because of the presence of the characters themselves. Then I went at writing it like that, in a very chaotic way at first, because I myself lost the thread many times, until, little by little, through the hard work of continuously rewriting, I started defining and polishing it all, as seen in the manuscripts that are in Princeton's archives.

Critics have asked me, "Did you write the story chronologically first and then cut it and mix it up?" No, absolutely not. I wrote the story in that unstructured way, from the point of view of chronology, and then I avoided jumps that were too brusque, that could break the continuity or lose the reader's attention. That technique seeks to maintain suspense, dislocating the reader in order to interest her more in what is happening, in what will happen, or in what has already happened. The events narrated in the story are realistic—some are very gruesome, others are very violent—because there is nothing that would not happen in reality. You can call it a realistic work, but only in its plot and characters, and not its structure, its construction.

DIEGO NEGRÓN-REICHARD: Did you know from the beginning how the story would end? Or did the plot change along the creative way?

MVLL: No, I had absolutely no idea. I knew I wanted to write a novel about Odría's dictatorship, which was more corrupt and corruptive than violent, although it was also violent. The story I wanted to tell was about how a dictatorship of that kind seeps into private lives to destroy relationships between fathers and sons, to destroy vocations, to frustrate people. I wanted to show how a dictatorship ends up demoralizing even those who are good deep inside, those who are decent by nature. If a good person wants to get ahead in this world, he is forced to make moral, civic, and political concessions. I wanted to narrate how this affects all levels of society: the oligarchy, the small sector of the middle class, but also the working class. I was interested in a portrait of society in which the political dictatorship has an effect on activities very removed from politics: family life, professional life, people's vocations. Politics infects everything and creates rifts in the hearts of families and in citizens themselves that would never have occurred without the corrupting force that is political power. That was my initial idea.

I made lots of notes. At the beginning, I wanted to tell that story through a bodyguard, a kind of henchman lacking in morality, who can defend or beat someone according to who pays him. And I thought that character, who is called Ambrosio in the novel, could be the good one. But later I realized no, there shouldn't be a main character, so that the story could be spread among many characters.

THE CHARACTERS

RG: The Spanish-Dominican critic Carlos Esteban Deive published an article that includes a directory of all the characters in *Conversation in The Cathedral*. It starts with the Zavala family and the other members of the bourgeoisie and goes on down, dividing the characters by profession and social class: government officials, journalists, police, workers, and on and on until it gets to henchmen and prostitutes. It comes to a total, in all, of seventy characters. How did you keep track of all those characters as you wrote the novel?

MVLL: Those characters represent the whole spectrum of Peruvian society of that time. I didn't have them all at first: they came up as the story needed to touch upon other places and cover other spaces from that world. Some are just passing through, and others are more permanent. But from the beginning, I did have that idea of a group that would show a society in flux, with its great contradictions, its great differences, its way of speaking, its language and expressions. That is how the characters started arising—except for the small group that is the most constant—as I developed the plots that in the end become one story.

RG: Marcel Proust's critics have devoted many books to investigating the "keys" to his characters, in other words, to identifying those friends of the novelist's who served as models. Proust objected that reality was much more complex and that what he created were amalgamations, taking, for example, the personality of one friend, the physical aspects of a relative, a phrase said by an acquaintance, and throwing all of that into one literary character. Are there models for the characters in *Conversation in The Cathedral?* Or are we dealing with, as in the case of Proust, amalgamations?

MVLL: Literary characters are always amalgamations. It's true that there are models taken from real life that function as a starting point for the author, because a being that is 100 percent invented does not exist. All authors have had at some point a model, although later, imagination and the development of the story itself go shaping the character, steering it in a certain way, giving it a certain psychology and way of speaking. There is an amalgamation process, because a novelist takes the eyes of one person, the hair of another, the ears of a third, and thus goes building it. In the end, it is that selection of components that lends originality to the creation, and that reflects the author's imagination. That is why you can never speak of a model that is absolutely real, although certain creations by the author can, as a starting point, be inspired by real live men and women. You have to remember that, ultimately, literary characters are made of words. There is such a chasm between a literary being and a real live person that no one should have the right to feel represented in a novel. Although some are based on real models, in literature they become others, pure verbal creations.

RG: In *Conversation in The Cathedral*, there are characters who speak, but there is no narrator who judges them or interprets the plot. I remember that in a text about *Tirant lo Blanc* you write that for a novel to work, the narrator should not judge its characters: it is they, who, through their actions and words, show what kind of people they are, whether good or bad, sincere or hypocritical.

MVLL: That's a Flaubertian idea, and it seems absolutely valid: the narrator should be like God and be with all of his characters, be present for everything that happens, but not be visible at any moment. He should be a very active force behind everything happening, but he should never interject to opine or judge, or interfere in the action, because the believability depends entirely on that neutrality. The narrator should not get involved with his emotions, with his judgments, with his prejudices, in the lives of his creations. That was the great lesson of *Madame Bovary*: one narrates, doesn't opine, doesn't argue, doesn't judge. That is the role of the narrator. I believe I have always followed that lesson, except for when I have a narrator who is also a character in the plot. If the one telling the story is a narrator of that sort, of course he can express his reactions, his judgments, and his prejudices: he opines from what he is, from the point of view of one more actor in the plot.

RG: In *Conversation in The Cathedral*, the characters all express value judgments about the other characters. For example, when Ambrosio talks to Santiago about Santiago's father, Santiago criticizes his father—he deems him a bourgeois, he deems him a hypocrite—while Ambrosio defends him.

MVLL: He defends him, in addition, with enormous respect.

Cayo Bermúdez

RG: In *A Fish in the Water*, you narrate an encounter you had, when you were studying at the university, with the person who inspired the character of Cayo Bermúdez, Odría's chief of police. Can you tell us about how you created that fictional character on the basis of that encounter?

MVLL: I began at the Universidad of San Marcos in the year 1953. At that moment, there were two universities in Peru: Universidad Católica and San Marcos, which was a public university and one of the two oldest in Latin America, along with the one in Santo Domingo. At San Marcos, people of modest means studied, while at Católica, there were kids from good families and from the upper-middle class. Those differences began to blur later, but at the time, they were very stark. I had always wanted to go to San Marcos, even against my family's desires, because I wanted to become closer to those opposing Odría's dictatorship.

I hated Odría and shared that hate with my family. When I was at school, I read a book that convinced me that the only serious way to fight for a different society, a just one, was by being communist. And since they said that San Marcos was a rebel university where the communists were, I wanted to go there. Then I entered San Marcos, which was, like all institutions in Peru, under strict government control. The dictatorship had undercover cops among the students, and we had to be very careful about what we said during our classes. It was one of the few institutions where there was real resistance to the dictatorship, to the degree that students were militant in two clandestine opposition parties. One of them, the majority one at the time, was the Aprista Party, which had a socialist orientation and suffered a lot of repression under the military governments. There were also the communists, who belonged to a very, very small party, in which I was a militant for a year. As a friend of mine used to say, we communists were "very few, but very sectarian." In our party cell at San Marcos, there were fifteen of us, and although there were no more than three Trotskyites, we would repeat the slogan "The main enemy is Trotskyism," in keeping with the Stalinist line.

There were so few of us because the Marxist Party had suffered terrible repression in the year 1952, because of a political strike organized at San Marcos. Almost all of our leaders were in prison or in exile, or had been killed. There were students imprisoned at the Panóptico, a jail in the middle of Lima, and one day we found out that they had them sleeping on the floor. We members of the Cahuide group, the name the Communist Party had at the time, decided to organize a collection to take some blankets to them. We managed to buy them and take them to the Panóptico, but the head of the prison said to us, "You can't give anything to the prisoners here if there's no order from the head of government," in other words, the head of state security, a nearly mythical person called Alejandro Esparza Zañartu. He was Odría's right hand. This man was very efficient in his work: he sent undercover cops to infiltrate the students at the university and did the same with the unions. He was the one who really controlled all of the dictatorship's repressive machinery.

We argued a lot in our cell over whether we were going to go ask the head of government to allow us to deliver the blankets. Finally, the majority voted in favor and we assembled a delegation of five students. We asked for an audience with Esparza Zañartu. He set a time and we went to the government ministry, which was in an old building in the city center. All of us were very unsettled because we didn't know if we would come out of that meeting, if they were going to lock us up in the Panóptico as well. After waiting, they had us enter an office where a character was sitting at his desk. And it turned out to be the fearsome head of security, who was a sickly little man, sunken in his chair. It was shocking to me to discover that he was so physically insignificant: his face was like parchment, and he wore a scowl. He didn't even greet us. He kept the five of us standing in front of his desk. We spoke as we had agreed: first one, then the other, explaining that we wanted to take some blankets to our colleagues because they had them sleeping on the floor. He didn't move, and looked at us without saying a word. I also looked at him and thought, "We're so afraid of this man, and look at what he is: he is a disgrace of a human being."

Suddenly, he opened a little drawer and took out a few mimeographed sheets and showed us an issue of *Cahuide*, the little clandestine newspaper that we communist students put out. We got very nervous because we all worked on that publication. Esparza Zañartu kept looking at us and said, "What about this? There's no issue that's not about me, so I'm very grateful to you for taking such good care of me. Is this what you go to the university for? To plan the communist revolution and insult me?" We were frozen because that man seemed to enjoy being omniscient. He knew everything we were doing. "I know where you meet," he was saying to us, "I know where the mimeographer is, I know where you put together this rag." I don't remember how the audience ended—I think in the end he gave us permission to take the blankets—but what I do remember is that I said to myself, "I have to write a story in which a character like this is central, because this very powerful man who puts people in jail and orders their deaths is a complete zero of a human."

That is how the idea came up of writing a story in which a character like him would be central. Many years went by, but when I finally wrote *Conversation in The Cathedral*, I did so with that encounter in mind. When the novel came out, journalists recognized Esparza Zañartu—at the time, he had come back from exile and was living in a little farmhouse on the outskirts of Lima—and they went to interview him and told him he was portrayed as Cayo Shithead in *Conversation in The Cathedral*. No one would have expected his response: "Hell," he told them, "if Vargas Llosa had come to see me, I would have told him more interesting things than what he put in his novel." Now I think that he was certainly right: if he had told me about all of the barbarities he committed, my character would have been even worse.

Carlitos

RG: There's a passage in which Carlitos, one of Zavalita's colleagues at *La Crónica*, complains about journalism. He says,

"You get in and you can't get out, it's quicksand . . . You keep on sinking, sinking. You hate it, you can't free yourself. You hate it and suddenly you're ready for anything just to get a scoop. Staying up all night, getting into incredible places. It's an addiction, Zavalita."

MVLL: Carlitos Ney is speaking not just about journalism, but also about himself, because he wanted to be a poet, but journalism ate up his life and swallowed it whole. Journalism, but also the bohemian life: he gets used to leaving the newsroom straight for the bar and becomes an alcoholic. He continued his vocation as a writer, but barely exercised it anymore. And in the end that kid, who had seemed like he was going to be an important poet, doesn't even end up publishing one book. That's why he has such a grudge, because he thinks that journalism is what brought him down. In reality, he brought himself down. Many young people wanted to be writers, poets, or novelists; they saw journalism as an activity that started breaking up their lives and ended up destroying that initial vocation in them.

Hortensia

RG: Hortensia is a fascinating character who allows us to see how politics has effects on the sectors of the population that lack political consciousness. How did you conceive of this character? At what point does she enter the novel?

MVLL: Hortensia is a character who is above what she is, because her life is very limited. She is a woman who sells her body for pleasure, but she is also someone who thinks, who has a perspective about what is happening. I wanted the Muse—who is a kind of more frivolous prostitute—to have someone in her circle who would be able to see her with a critical eye, who would be able to take a certain distance upon observing her in her relationship with Cayo Bermúdez. Hortensia opens the door to that intimacy where the reader discovers what is really happening between Ambrosio and the Muse. In addition to being a prostitute, she needed to be intelligent, delicate, and capable of introducing a violent, bloody, and criminal episode. She inhabits the darkest part of the novel, because of the enormous violence she represents. But Hortensia is a very ambiguous character: she is not educated, but she does have natural intelligence that allows her to make very sound observations about her surroundings and about the characters with whom she deals.

RG: In *Conversation in The Cathedral*, political life even enters the bedroom and influences the characters' sex lives.

MVLL: I was interested in analyzing how sex can turn into a kind of escape route. Repression creates an asphyxiating climate that stimulates sexual activity because people seek a kind of subterfuge in intimacy to escape the claustrophobia in which they live. Sex lives are exacerbated in a society that is overwhelmed by a dictatorship.

RG: There are historical events that occur in the novel—for example, the strike in Arequipa—that readers see through Hortensia's eyes. There are many political interests in that strike, but Hortensia sees it in a more personal and more direct way: if the strikers manage to overthrow Cayo, she'll be left without any money.

BEN HUMMEL: Queta seems like a more frivolous character than Hortensia, but she has moments of great lucidity. There's a moment in which she says, "I'm more disgusted by Gold Ball than by Cayo." That's very perceptive: Cayo is evil, but at least he acts in accordance with his evilness, whereas Don Fermín presents himself as good while hiding a very corrupt, very dark personality.

MVLL: Of course, because Don Fermín is a hypocrite. He has the appearance of a respectable gentleman, but he leads a life that is not at all respectable and that is full of secrets.

DN: Hortensia seems to have a democratizing effect: all who come to her house—be they rich or poor, powerful or weak—become equals. All drink, dance, and participate in orgies. It is as if Hortensia's house were an egalitarian space that forces everyone to relate to one another on the same level, and she achieves that through her sexuality.

MARLIS HINCKLEY: There's an ambiguity in Hortensia's character: she thinks that the parties are for her and for Queta, but we know that Cayo uses them to do politics by other means. How much control does Hortensia have over her life? Or is she simply a pawn in Cayo's game?

MVLL: Hortensia comes to have certain influence without a doubt, but at the same time she is very naïve. She thinks she is worthy on her own, when really her worth comes from the power Cayo Bermúdez gives her, which he uses as well for his own means. She is able to see beyond that and to have a perspective about what is happening around her. Her testimony is important: she has her own personal interests, which are very, very small, but that does not prevent her from having a broader vision of the characters surrounding her. She comes to have certain power because of what she knows, what she has said, what she has experienced. That is why she becomes dangerous, and that is why they kill her.

RG: I imagine that the character of Hortensia came about, in part, from your experience at *La Crónica* and your participation in that world, where there were rumors constantly going around about the sex life of politicians and Peru's most powerful men.

MVLL: Absolutely: it's something that frequently occurs in repressive societies. When you can't talk about something, people give free rein to their imaginations: censorship becomes a big incentive for unbridled fantasy. Dirty conversations and sex-themed jokes occur in a way that is inversely proportional to the repression that dominates official life, in which those subjects are not discussed or even mentioned. Repression generates an increase in curiosity and insults. That constantly occurs in *Conversation in The Cathedral*.

DN: Hortensia's character also shows us another aspect of Cayo Bermúdez's personality. Cayo always appears to be uninterested, listless, when dealing with political or even economic matters. The only time in which he shows sincere interest is when he visits Hortensia. It's as if in that house, he is allowed to live out passions to which he has no access in other dimensions of his life.

MVLL: Cayo Bermúdez lives in a profoundly male-chauvinistic society. He wants to feel important and powerful, and having a lover like Hortensia makes him feel he has moved up on the social pyramid, that he has reached the stature of a real man. In a chauvinistic society, to have lovers—especially beautiful lovers—means to have arrived at a social and economic level that he couldn't even have dreamed of when he was a wine vendor.

The interesting thing about Cayo is that he never imagined he would come to have so much power. He is a man who "met his fate," to use a phrase by Borges: he was an obscure character, a merchant in a minor province. But his buddy, who becomes the president of the republic, calls him one day to offer him the post of government administrator: a small, bureaucratic post that Cayo turns into a position of great power, from which repression is exercised and upon which the regime's survival comes to depend. Thus, the poor devil turns into a man of utmost importance. He was a nobody, he didn't exist, he was a small merchant who had no luck in business and had married the milkmaid's daughter, an ugly woman who didn't love him. And he goes on to be a feared, hated man who has the power to decide the lives, freedoms, and deaths of many Peruvians. He consolidates all of that for himself, paying for a high-class lover, because Hortensia isn't just any lover. You couldn't say that he is in love with her or anything close to it: she is an object of pleasure that makes him feel powerful, above his origins, above his social class. All of that is easier to understand in the context of a society with great inequalities, of a society ruled by machismo, that is going through terrible repression.

VICTORIA NAVARRO: Hortensia is a character that reminds me of Doña Adriana in *Palomino Molero*: they are both women living in a world of machismo who have to appropriate the instruments of machismo in order to survive.

MVLL: In a chauvinistic society, the woman is a victim in the sexual arena, but at the same time she has privileges. Machismo turns a woman into a parasite: she has to be kept because she shouldn't study or work. In the era in which the novel takes place, it was viewed poorly for a woman to work: only those in the lower classes worked, not a decent woman who should mind her house and her children. If she belonged to the upper-middle class, she had to be very well kept. She had to be faithful, decent, respectable, but her husband—if he had money—could have lovers. Machismo distorts everything and changes the shape of reality. Sometimes, women accept the condition imposed on them by society and confirm it by their behavior, by their way of being. Hortensia and Adriana are two marginal figures in that world. Adriana is a woman of very modest means, from the countryside. Hortensia belongs to the lower-middle class, much higher than Doña Adriana. Her life is based on machismo: machismo exploits her and, in the end, kills her, but it also gives her money, jewels, dresses, prestige. Machismo deeply distorts human relations, among men as well as women.

Amalia

LARA NORGAARD: Continuing on the theme of women from the working class in the novel, Amalia, the maid, is another very important character. She is very conservative and comes from a very traditional world, especially regarding sexual matters, but despite her prejudices, she goes to work at Hortensia's house and develops deep affection for her.

MVLL: Amalia admires the woman, and, in a way, loves her. But it is an unequal relationship, because to Hortensia, Amalia is a maid and will continue being so until the end. This is a fairly typical attitude: slaves love their masters even though the masters exploit them. It's a very generalized defense mechanism: a maid loves her mistress because if she hated her, she would feel much worse. Loving and admiring that person makes her servile condition more bearable.

Amalia doesn't really understand what is happening: she's very modest and her values make her see the world from a very limited perspective. To her, Hortensia is a grand dame, although the reader knows that a grand dame wouldn't deign to give Hortensia a passing glance. Amalia sees in Hortensia a woman who wears expensive clothing, who receives important people at her house, someone who has reached the pinnacle of society. Her perspective is very different from that of other characters.

RG: There is a very entertaining literary game because the character of Amalia, who comes from a very conservative world, is the voice that narrates the parties and orgies that Hortensia throws, but from a very prudish point of view.

MVLL: Amalia doesn't understand many things. She narrates them but without understanding them. The one who does understand is the reader.

RG: Amalia's perspective is marked by many contradictions: she has a very petit bourgeois morality, but she relays the most perverse and denigrating scenes, which seem normal to her because of the admiration she feels for Hortensia.

MVLL: Exactly. The same thing occurs in the case of Ambrosio and Fermín. Ambrosio should hate Fermín, who is the man who exploits him, both sexually and as a laborer, but things don't happen that way. Ambrosio has a nearly religious admiration for Don Fermín and feels privileged thanks to the intimacy that Don Fermín has bestowed upon him. That is why the relationship between Amalia and Hortensia is similar to that between Ambrosio and Don Fermín.

Ivonne

JENNIFER SHYUE: There is a difference between Hortensia's house and Ivonne's house, which is another space where we see how machismo works.

MVLL: Ivonne's house is a high-class whorehouse. In the Peru of that time, there were modest whorehouses but also elegant ones, for people who had more money.

I'd like to point out that today's Peru is not as backward as the world in *Conversation in The Cathedral*. Today, girls from bourgeois families go to the university, become professionals, participate in society's economic sphere, and in some cases come to have important leadership roles. All of this was impossible in the 1950s. There has been considerable evolution in many fields. We're still very far from an absolutely egalitarian society between men and women, which still doesn't exist, not even in the most advanced countries. There is still a certain lag. Machismo goes back to the beginning of time; it is still a force even in the most modern societies.

Aída

LN: Aída is the only woman in the novel who is neither bourgeois nor a prostitute.

MVLL: She is a political activist, she wants to change things, she acts in a world that is very marked by men.

LN: Yes, but she also appears as an object, because Santiago is in love with her, and so is Jacobo: her main role in the novel is to be the woman desired by two men who later compete to see who gets her. Aída seems to be the strongest woman in the book, but she also ends up being an object over which the two male characters fight.

MVLL: We're getting into very controversial terrain there. Aída is a person who is very conscious of what is wrong in her society and who wants to act—she becomes an activist. Well then, does that prevent her from falling in love?

LN: Of course not: she can fall in love, and she does fall in love. But the interesting thing is that all of the novel's women fall in love with someone, while the men do not: there are male characters who walk through the novel without falling in love with anyone.

MVLL: In Aída's case, there are two who fall in love with her. In the end, she picks one.

LN: Yes.

MVLL: Let's hope they were happy!

SPACES IN THE NOVEL

La Crónica

LN: I wanted to ask you a question about *La Crónica*, the newspaper where Zavalita works in *Conversation*. This is a not very serious or sophisticated daily, and it publishes sensationalist pieces. Would you say that the daily is apolitical? Or could we say that this type of journalism also has a political dimension?

MVLL: That's a very interesting question. Is it possible to find a completely apolitical newspaper? The regime's objective, not just under Odría's dictatorship but under all dictatorships, is to get the population to entirely lose interest in politics, to renounce political life and to let this remain in the hands of those in power. The surest way to have a calm life in Odría's Peru was to abstain from politics. This was the function of *La Crónica* and all newspapers of the time, which didn't mention a subject, or if they did, they tried to do so in a way that would not be controversial or generate a variety of reactions. For example, it was reported, "The minister made certain decrees." If there was some political incident, it was silenced.

In Odría's Peru, political life simply didn't exist. The Law for the Safety of the Republic forbade all political parties, and as such, there was no official political life. Politics was the realm of the government, and the government simply issued decrees. I remember that a year before I joined *La Crónica*, during my school vacation, I worked at my father's office. He was the director of a U.S. agency called International News Service, which was later folded into United Press. I acted as messenger: I took the news from the Inter-

national News Service office to *La Crónica*, which had a monopoly on that agency. I remember there was an instruction
sheet on the wall for the news staff that said, "All news that
comes from abroad and refers directly or indirectly to Peru
should go through the government ministry before being
taken to *La Crónica*." Each piece of news having to do with
Peru required the approval of the ministry's censor. In other
words, articles from the international agencies reached
the newspaper censored already, purged of everything that
irritated those in power. And no newspaper of the time
would publish, of its own initiative, any criticism of the
government.

In the 1950s, the whole press was in the hands of very
economically powerful families. *La Crónica* belonged to the
Prados, a very rich family who owned banks and many indus-
tries; *La Prensa* was the property of Pedro Beltrán, a landowner. And *El Comercio* belonged to the Miró Quesada
family. These three families from the oligarchy were very
close to the dictatorship, and censorship was exercised in mu-
tual agreement.

What I recall from my youth, and what is portrayed in
Conversation in The Cathedral, is a country where young people lived in a world where the only way to be political was by
adopting subversive strategies, going clandestine, or joining
parties that were illegal. In that world, newspapers were not
a source of information and readers knew that nothing was
discussed there that was important in the political arena. And
the same thing happened with radio. We lived in absolute
ignorance of what was happening in the country, a situation
that made anxious young people despair since they intuited,
besides, that Peru was not where it should be to be a modern
and democratic country. We lived in a climate of despair, of

being downtrodden, of being demoralized, which is what I try to reflect in the novel.

RG: We know what kind of articles Zavalita writes for *La Crónica* in the novel. Can you tell us about the articles you wrote in the months you worked for *La Crónica*?

MVLL: I remember some of the articles I wrote for the page where the staff had the right to sign their names, because at *La Crónica* we didn't normally sign our articles, except for on the weekly collaborations that tended to be more personal. I remember, for example, one about the *cachascán*, which was a variation of the *lucha libre*, very in vogue at the time: I went to many of those sporting events. I also remember one about the theater, which was a very minor and marginal activity in the Peru of that time. In Juan Gargurevich's book *Mario Vargas Llosa: Reportero a los quince años* (Mario Vargas Llosa: Fifteen-year-old reporter), a few more I had forgotten about appear: a report about tuberculosis, another one about pharmacies that sold expired medications.

LN: In Peru, there were different kinds of newspapers, some more serious than others. *La Crónica* is a daily that I would classify as sensationalist.

MVLL: Sensationalist journalism looks like literature: there is an element of fantasy, of the grotesque and the ridiculous. Serious journalism seeks to express a reality, while sensationalist journalism reshapes reality to make it more attractive and more interesting to its audience. That is why sensationalist journalism, yellow journalism, is closer to literature than to objective journalism.

When I worked at *La Crónica*, the model was U.S. journalism, with its insistence on the famous lede. You had to begin the news piece by putting key information in the first two lines to then develop the most important event from which the rest of the news was derived. In that sense, the most modern newspaper in Peru was not *La Crónica*, but *La Prensa*, which was the first to publish those kinds of reports. Although there was a precept of U.S. journalism that neither *La Prensa* nor any other newspaper could fulfill: the requirement of presenting the information with absolute objectivity, without opining—except on the editorial page—as if the article were a screen placed over reality. This was a chimera in a country where there was no freedom.

It is worth remembering that sensationalist journalism has always existed. Along with journalism is born a tendency to turn reporting into something more than mere information to awaken curiosity in the public: details are highlighted that have a certain distance from reality and that end up giving disproportionate importance to certain eccentric facts. This is a genre that has always existed but was marginal for a long time. Gossip journalism, for example, publishes details belonging to people's private lives that should not be made public under normal circumstances. There has always been a morbid curiosity about the private lives of politicians, artists, public figures, and other personalities. But for quite a few years now, sensationalist journalism has become more and more important, and today we have a press that specializes in yellow journalism. This has taken on such importance that it has become difficult to distinguish, as before, between serious journalism and yellow journalism. Sensationalism creeps into the most serious magazines and newspapers. Why? Because there is public pressure for journalism to also be entertainment, even if it means gossip that invades people's private lives. It is a phenomenon of our time that occurs as much in the underdeveloped world as in the developed world, in less educated countries as in more educated countries.

In *Conversation in The Cathedral*, the phenomenon of yellow journalism is already beginning to insinuate itself. Could we conclude that yellow journalism is born in the Third World? That, I really don't know.

RG: In *Conversation*, the journalists all lead very frivolous lives. Zavalita and his colleagues go straight from the newsroom to cabarets and brothels.

MVLL: At that time, journalism and a bohemian nightlife were inseparable. It was night work, and journalists cohabitated with other nocturnal dwellers: people at bars, at nightclubs, at cabarets, at whorehouses. That is the journalistic world I knew. Journalists stayed in the newsroom until the first issue of the paper came out, around twelve or one in the morning, and then they went to the bars to meet up with their colleagues from other papers. Some were great drinkers, and often the nights ended at the whorehouses. The journalist is a key figure in nightlife. That has changed a lot now, but at the time it was like that.

There's a little book by Ricardo Palma, a nineteenth-century Peruvian writer, called *La bohemia de mi tiempo* (The bohemia of my time), and it portrays a world of poets and writers who were all journalists. They all earned a living doing reporting and, as happened when I started working at *La Crónica*, they spent the night, after coming out of the newsroom, at the bar. Journalism was one of the manifestations of the bohemian life and an important component of nightlife. Afterward, things changed and journalism came to be a profession like any other, taught at universities or specialized schools. At the time, one became a journalist by working in a newsroom. Many intellectuals and writers worked as journalists because it was a way of earning a living.

PABLO GUTIÉRREZ: A key difference between Zavalita and Mario Vargas Llosa is that Vargas Llosa was able to get out of Lima's journalism world. As you tell it in *A Fish in the Water*, the moment came in which you took the risk of leaving Peru behind and went to study in Europe. Do you think that if you had stayed in Peru, your life would have ended up like Zavalita's, in other words, a great disappointment?

MVLL: You can never know how life would have been under different circumstances: that type of hypothesis can be neither verified nor refuted. I always dreamed of leaving Peru because I thought that if I stayed there, I would never come to be a writer, at least not how I thought a writer should be, devoted heart and soul to his vocation, and placing his writing above everything, devoting the best of his time, of his energy, to literature. In Peru, it would have been impossible for me to organize my life that way: I would have had to have all kinds of jobs to survive. My plan was to escape, get out, and I managed it thanks to a scholarship. Things abroad started coming together in such a way that I was really able to exercise my vocation. Perhaps I was naïve in thinking that I would achieve this only by leaving, because there are writers who didn't leave, who were very good writers and who managed to organize their lives in Peru. But for me, the idea of going to Europe was so important that if I hadn't gone, I probably would have felt very psychologically frustrated and could have ended up like Zavalita.

The Negro–Negro

LN: There's an interesting detail relating to U.S. journalism that appears in *Conversation*. One of the cabarets, the Negro-Negro, has a wall covered with covers of *The New Yorker* magazine. When Carlitos talks about his frustration with the world of journalism, Zavalita observes him and looks at his face with that background of magazines, as if *The New Yorker* represented a kind of serious, intellectual journalism that Carlitos would never be able to reach.

MVLL: To Zavalita, *The New Yorker* represents the existence of life outside Peru: a world without a dictatorship, without censorship, without all of the great traumas he is living through in his own country.

LN: The covers of *The New Yorker* appear twice: first, in that scene with Carlitos, and later, toward the end of the novel, when Zavalita finds out about the relationship between his father and Ambrosio and he goes to the Negro-Negro to distract himself. The description is nearly the same: the covers are "brilliant, ironic, multicolored."

MIGUEL CABALLERO-VÁZQUEZ: Those *New Yorker* covers give us the impression that news from outside did reach Peru during Odría's dictatorship. It is as if censorship didn't touch what came from outside, as if the foreign press was no threat.

MVLL: In those years, Peru was experiencing something very typical of dictatorships: a great nationalist exaltation that presents anything homegrown as a value in and of itself. But there was also, among the people, a real ignorance of what was really happening outside. The majority of the population had acquired the second nature that consists of not being interested in what they don't have, with the exception of the most educated and the most idealistic groups, who were very much a fringe minority. From an economic viewpoint, those were good years for Peru: the increase in the value of raw materials in the international market produced general economic improvement, which the dictatorship really took advantage of to promote itself.

MCV: Was there some country that was the model of what Odría's Peru didn't want to be?

MVLL: There was a right wing whose main desire was to maintain order and protect its economic interests. It wasn't the classic, refined right, nor was it an educated bourgeoisie; rather, it was quite the opposite. The rich in Peru were very unrefined people: whiskey was their only culture, and their main concern was making money. The same thing was happening in almost all of Latin America's countries, with the exceptions of Argentina and Chile, which did have an educated bourgeoisie.

The left, by contrast, was paralyzed by dogmatic Marxism. Its model was the Soviet Union, and this lasted until the outbreak of the Cuban Revolution, when suddenly, a new model appeared for the Latin American left. But that didn't happen until 1959.

In the years I narrate in *Conversation*, there were only two models for the countries of Latin America: dictatorship or Stalinism.

THE END

RG: The end of *Conversation in The Cathedral* is one of the saddest and most full of despair in literature. Ambrosio finishes relaying his life, where everything has gone from bad to worse as he sinks into greater and greater poverty and ever more serious moral degradation, until in the end he says that when his contract at the dog pound is up, he's going to look for another job and then die.

MVLL: It's the beginning of the novel, but the beginning is also how the novel concludes.

RG: It is a very pessimistic ending, in which there seems to be no way to escape the corrupting effects of the dictatorship.

MVLL: Throughout the novel, there is a climate of deception, a disillusionment with the country's situation. In Santiago's case, this feeling directly affects his family life. His father is a person who is linked to the regime, who receives the dictatorship's support for his business, and this gives the kid, who is becoming conscious of his country's social and political problems, one more reason to feel demoralized, depressed. I think this is the ambience that fills the whole novel: the climate of disillusionment that my entire generation lived because we began our adult lives very young, in a country where there was no free press, where there was no political life.

RG: Does the novel's pessimism correspond to the emotional state you lived in while writing it?

MVLL: I always say that all of my gray hairs come from that novel. I spent more than three years and a lot of work on writing it. At the beginning, I felt that I was doing so blind, narrating stories and relaying episodes without knowing how they would connect. When I had an idea of the structure, of that main conversation, it was then less of a tangle for me to work. But it was very hard for me and I felt great relief when I finally finished.

The novel was not successful, especially when you compare it to other books of mine, precisely because of the difficulty. Oddly, it has earned more and more readers over time; it has been republished and now is more alive than other books of mine. It has conquered readers little by little. I find that very encouraging. If you rank the things I have written, that book should be among the top.

BEYOND THE NOVEL

DIEGO VIVES: Thinking about the pessimistic vision that appears in *Conversation in The Cathedral*, could you talk about how your vision of Peru evolves throughout your work?

MVLL: I was very pessimistic when I wrote *Conversation in The Cathedral*. I had very little hope that Peru would come out of the well it was in. That vision has changed over time. In my last books—*The Discreet Hero* and *The Neighborhood*—there is a vision of Peru that is less pessimistic, even optimistic.

Peru nowadays and the Peru from *Conversation in The Cathedral* are very different, for the better, fortunately. At that time there was a dictatorship; now there is a democracy that can be imperfect but that is preferable to the previous system. We have a degree of freedom of information and of criticism that was inconceivable at that time. A young Peruvian person today knows exactly what the world he lives in is like and can give his opinion without fear of reprisals. There are opportunities that are open to many more citizens than before, although not to everyone, because there is a peasant sector that is still very marginalized. But in general the population has greater opportunities, and this has given democracy a much wider support base. There are many hopes—for example, the idea of revolution—that have been extinguished to the point of being relegated to very minor sectors. Today, Peruvians have different ideas about the kind of society they desire, but there is a consensus in favor of democracy. That has generated a political and social stability that has led to greater development. There is a lot left to be done, without a doubt, but we can't deny that there is considerable progress, and that makes me less pessimistic than I was when I wrote *Conversation in The Cathedral*.

MCV: In the context of a political situation that has improved so much, what does a writer do to not lose his energy, his passion, his fury? *Conversation in The Cathedral* is a great novel in part because of the rage it expresses against injustice and corruption.

MVLL: Well, I think that in any situation there are subjects that can really stimulate creativity. What makes no sense is clinging to a reality that no longer exists. To describe a problem that has been phased out is to make literature that is already born dead. It's very difficult for someone to identify with a description of a current reality that doesn't match the experience of the present at all. There is a lot of literature that fails because of the disconnect between what it tells and what the reader is living. That is why it is so important for literature to express the living world. Even historical novels, if they lack that grain of lived reality, are born dead. But the literary vision of reality always transcends it, because it is never a mere photographic description of what is lived. Good literature adds something more to reality, but respects that secret contract between reader and author: "You're going to invent the story you want me to believe on the basis of the world we're living in."

MCV: I ask myself if *Conversation*, in addition to telling a complex story, sets out to teach the reader a critical way of looking at reality. That disordered narrative universe goes against the image of reality, simple and orderly, with good guys and bad guys, that a dictatorship projects.

MVLL: Yes, good novels teach us to look at reality in a more complex way. Great novels show us that mere appearances don't tell us everything, that the surface is very deceiving, and that to understand the world, you have to search deeply to discover the mechanisms behind behavior, behind events. Literature generates pleasure, it makes us enjoy, it shows us the immense possibilities of language, but at the same time, it makes us skeptical toward reality. It induces us to try to go beyond appearances to see what is behind a social event, a political event, a personal event. That is a function not just of literature but of art in general. All creative manifestations of culture have that effect on us: they make us less naïve when it comes to observing reality, when it comes to judging reality.

RG: That is one of Sartre's theses about engaged literature: the true political value of literature is not in the didactic message of socialist realism, but in the reading experience that leads the reader to a greater degree of consciousness, of understanding, and of critical awakening.

MVLL: That is the great idea of existentialism, which left a mark on me and on my entire generation. Sartre showed that literature is not gratuitous pleasure, but rather an instrument that arms the reader to understand reality, because it broadens her ethical vision, her moral vision. That is why literature in particular and culture in general turn out to be indispensable.

4

THE REAL LIFE OF ALEJANDRO MAYTA

The Real Life of Alejandro Mayta (1984) tells the story of an old revolutionary who failed in his attempt to launch an armed insurrection. It is the most detailed portrait that Mario Vargas Llosa has done of a leftist militant who bets on violent methods to make revolution. Playing with the genre of the detective novel, the narrator tries to reconstruct Mayta's life by interviewing his friends, family members, and accomplices until—in the final chapter—the old revolutionary surprisingly appears and gives a final testimony about his life.

RUBÉN GALLO: *The Real Life of Alejandro Mayta*, like *The War of the End of the World*, is based on a historic event. This time, we're dealing with an attempt at a rebellion that occurred in a city in the provinces in 1962. Why did you choose that episode as the novel's starting point?

MARIO VARGAS LLOSA: In the 1960s, I was living in Paris and learned of a minor episode that had occurred in Peru that really shocked me. The protagonist was an old Peruvian revolutionary militant who had been pro-APRA, then communist, and in the end—fed up with the communists' sectarianism and dogmatism—he turned Trotskyite.

The great conflict between Lenin and Trotsky, who had always been colleagues, centers around the future of the revolution. Lenin resigned himself to the fact that only one revolution existed—in the Soviet Union—while Trotsky wanted to continue working to make world revolution: the "permanent revolution," as he called it. Trotskyism came to be a very strong tendency in Latin America, through small parties that hated the official communist parties. In Peru, the Trotskyites called the Communist Party *rabanitos* (little radishes), red on the outside and white on the inside, because many were middle-class intellectuals, in contrast to the Trotskyites, who generally came from working-class families.

So in Paris I find out the story of Mayta, that old Trotskyite who had gone through all of Peru's leftist groups and who had brought together a small party called the Revolutionary Workers' Party T—the *T* was an apocope for "Trotskyite." At a party, that gentleman hears a young man speaking very eloquently and self-assuredly about armed revolution. And the old man thinks, "Look, here we have a young conqueror. He doesn't know anything, but he has great enthusiasm." But to his great surprise, he discovers that the young man speaking of revolution, whose name is Vallejos, is a police lieutenant. Then Mayta starts to get together with this young man and tries to indoctrinate him, to win him over to his cause, giving him pamphlets on Marxism. And what happens is the opposite.

Old Mayta doesn't manage to win over the young man, but the young man ends up seducing him, convincing him that revolution is possible, that in reality it is a waste of time to keep up with that union work, trying to win elections, because the leftist parties will never have enough money to gain the presidency. What they have to do is go out to the hills, start shooting, and mobilize the exploited people.

All of this occurs just a few years after the Cuban revolutionaries come down from the Sierra Maestra and take Havana. Then old Mayta becomes enthusiastic because, for the first time, he has the possibility of acting. He had spent his whole life handing out flyers, mobilizing unions, organizing strikes, and spending stints in jail every time he was caught. And suddenly, thanks to the enthusiasm of that young officer, he has the opportunity to plan the revolution. They decide that the insurrection should take place in Jauja, the first capital in the colonial period and also a city with symbolic importance for Peru because it is associated with wealth, with gold, with the mines: the Spanish settled there, in the middle of the mountains, but soon discovered that they were very isolated, surrounded by enormous masses of Indians, so they moved to the coast.

The young man meets several soldiers who support his plan, and they manage to convince a handful of sympathizers but don't obtain the support of the Communist Party, whose members want nothing to do with the Trotskyites. Lieutenant Vallejos, who was assigned to Jauja and had links with the Colegio Nacional in that city, brings in many students who would become clandestine messengers between the guerrilla nucleus and the support bases in the cities.

When the day comes to launch the revolution, all of the conspirators disappear: it turns out that no one wants to risk his life. So Mayta and Vallejos, the Trotskyite and the young officer, in an act of true madness, decide to launch the battle on their own, with the support of only a handful of students from Jauja's Colegio Nacional. And they do so. They attack the police, they take the rifles—although they have never seen weapons in their lives—and they go out to the countryside. The police immediately mobilize and squash the rebellion in the outskirts of Jauja. There, Vallejos and many students die. Mayta is wounded and left for dead.

This story was barely told in Peru because it was considered a very minor criminal event: it was not seen as an attempt at revolution. This episode made an impression on me and I was interested in the character of Mayta, that old Trotskyite: a man who spent his whole life going in and out of jail, devoted to a revolution he intuited was impossible, and, suddenly, thanks to that irresponsible and amateur young man who knew nothing of Marxism but who was overflowing with enthusiasm, he launches a revolutionary struggle that lasts just a few hours and ends in a big massacre.

So I set out to write that old Trotskyite's story. I changed his name to Mayta, which wasn't his actual name.

RG: Can you tell us about the research methods you used as you put together the novel?

MVLL: At first, I wanted to tell the story of the meeting with the soldier, focusing on the way that the young man seduced the old revolutionary and also telling about the intrigues to put together the operation and the tragic failure of the revolution. But when I started to investigate and gathered testimonies from people who knew them, I realized that everything they were telling me was lies: it was obvious that the witnesses were falsifying reality in order to justify themselves.

In the first place, all of them had committed themselves to the conspiracy but later got scared and withdrew. They told different stories, outrageous, absurd, false. It was flagrant, and all you had to do was compare and contrast them to re-alize they were exaggerating or lying. And that changed my novel along the way. In the end, it was turning into *stories* of Mayta, not just *the story* of Mayta, into different versions people gave about what had happened, which also proved the relativity of historic testimonies and the impossibility of es-tablishing an objective truth on the basis of witnesses' and protagonists' subjective versions.

No one knew what had happened to Mayta: he had dis-appeared. So I worked on the novel with the idea in mind that the main character of my story had either died or at least gone abroad without a trace. When I had practically finished the novel, I found out that Mayta was not only alive but in Lima: for ten years, he had been at Lurigancho, Lima's most well-known prison at the time.

I did the paperwork and obtained a permit to go into Lurigancho, and once there, I was told that Mayta had just left because he had finished serving his ten-year sentence. I met with the warden, who put me in touch with an inmate who was Mayta's best friend and who had a little fruit stand inside the prison. I spoke to that prisoner, who was very mis-trustful. I told him I was writing a book about his friend and that I was extremely interested in hearing his own testimony. Finally, I convinced him. He told me, "Yes. I'm going to tell you where to find him. He's working at an ice cream shop. He's been given a little stand selling ice creams in Mira-flores," which was the neighborhood where I was living.

From the prison, I went running straight to that ice cream stand. When I entered, I saw a man and knew it was him. I have never in my life seen such a face of stupefaction as that man's when I went up to him and said, "Look, I'm Mario Vargas Llosa. For two years, all I've been doing is thinking about you, imagining you, researching your life." He widened his eyes, looking at me as if I were mad, because you could tell he didn't believe anything I was telling him. I kept explaining. I told him, "Look, I'm writing a novel based on your story, on something I think is your story, because the reports I've been able to find are so contradictory that I no longer know which is your story. And that is why I would really like it if we could talk."

At the beginning, he seemed very mistrustful. He was a sick man, beaten, destroyed by life. Then he told me the following, which I relay in the last chapter of the book: "Well," he said to me, "I'm going to give you one night and that's it. Nothing more. And then we won't see each other again. Never again. On that night, I will tell you everything I remember."

I invited him to my house and we talked until dawn. It was a very shocking conversation that lasted about eight hours, and the one I give a literary version of in the book. He wrote my last chapter. I had thought of ending it a very different way, but his sudden appearance made me change the novel completely. What did I discover in that conversation? Something unexpected: that I knew more about the story of Jauja than he did. To him, Jauja was one episode of many—and not the most important one—in a long and complicated life.

What I did establish was that after Jauja, he had been imprisoned and released. Starting with his release, he had devoted himself to purely criminal activities that could no longer be justified by revolution or politics. His last sentence had been for an armed assault on a shoe store that had left one person dead. So that old revolutionary had ended up a common criminal.

He remembered a lot about that prior period, but Jauja had been left behind. In addition, he was unaware of many things. I had to constantly correct him. I showed him newspaper clippings that he hadn't seen, in which they presented the rebellion as a raid, as a problem involving thieves who attacked the police because they wanted to steal some llamas from there.

He looked at all of this information in absolute wonder. And he was very sick: he was an aged man, very thin, who coughed nonstop. He spent the night coughing, drinking water, going to urinate. Prison had wasted him away.

It made quite an impression on me that politics no longer interested him at all: revolutionary combat had been eclipsed from his memory. The only thing in his life that made him proud was that little fruit stand he'd put together with his friend in prison. He spoke with great pride and said, "We would clean the fruit. We always sold it all clean. And people trusted us, besides. So much so that others gave us their money to watch over. The miscreants, the criminals who were in jail, the ones who hacked each other to death, they respected us and gave us their money to watch over. We took on the role of a bank for them." And that was the best credential he presented to me. To me, it seemed pathetic that the Trotskyite revolutionary no longer remembered his theoretical readings or even Trotsky. That is the story of Mayta.

When the book was published, *Caretas* magazine, in Lima, searched the archives and published a photo of Mayta in the Jauja days. But I never learned what his reaction was, because I never saw him again or received any word of him. I don't know what happened to him, whether he stayed in Peru, whether he went back to prison. I don't even know if he read the book.

THE HISTORICAL CONTEXT

RG: Can we talk for a moment about what happened in the Jauja rebellion? It was summer of 1962, after the end of Odría's dictatorship and the elections that brought Manuel Prado to the presidency. The Cuban Revolution had triumphed, its leaders had been in power for three years, and the Cuban Missile Crisis had yet to happen. The Latin American political scene had changed a lot, and Peru was living a very different moment from the one you portray in *Conversation in The Cathedral.*

MVLL: Before the Cuban Revolution, there were many revolutionary attempts that failed. At that time, the Communist Party had a nearly complete monopoly on Marxism. There were socialist parties that followed a peaceful tendency and even, in some cases, a democratic one: they believed in elections, they believed you could achieve socialism through the vote or through a parliamentary majority. But the communist parties had a monopoly on Marxism. Certain big countries, like Mexico, had a Communist Party that was a real political power: an important party, with representation in the chambers, that had great influence in union struggles.

In other Latin American countries—governed by dictatorships, military juntas, or right-wing governments—communist parties were forbidden: they existed, but only clandestinely because the pressure of the United States was great. These were the Cold War years, and there was an anti-communist U.S. policy that demanded the participation of Latin American governments in that battle. Communist parties, meanwhile, were an instrument of the Soviet Union:

they depended completely upon the USSR, which subsidized them and gave them clear infrastructure.

It is important to highlight that these parties didn't believe in democracy, because it seemed to them that this was one of the masks of exploitation, and they thought that a democratic system would never resolve basic problems of justice, of great economic inequalities, affecting the Third World. In Peru, the PCP—the Peruvian Communist Party—was so small in part because it competed with the APRA—the American Popular Revolutionary Alliance—founded by Víctor Raúl Haya de la Torre with the ambition of being not just a Peruvian party but a Latin American one. Haya de la Torre was a Peruvian of aristocratic origins—of a very impoverished aristocracy—who was born in a province in the country's north. He was a great speaker, with enormous charisma. The APRA became a very popular party with an important peasant and worker base. This greatly stalled the growth of the Communist Party. In addition, the APRA earned the respect of a large part of the population because it confronted the military and launched an attack against the barracks in the city of Trujillo. The dictator Sánchez Cerro, a soldier, unleashed ghastly repression and ordered the executions of hundreds of APRA-ists in the pre-Inca ruins of Chan Chan, which were bathed in blood, according to legend.

All of this gave the APRA a lot of prestige and a lot of power, and caused great rivalry between this party and that of the communists. This is an important antecedent because prior to the triumph of the Cuban Revolution in 1959, Latin America had not had a single triumphant revolution. The communist parties that were working legally, where they could, proposed a great alliance of left-wing forces to work within the democratic system and undermine it from within.

The Cuban Revolution changed the panorama: for the first time in the history of Latin America, a leftist movement went to the mountains and survived, despite all attempts to squash it. It grew, prospered, and eventually succeeded in bringing down the Batista regime and establishing the first revolutionary government in Latin America, something that created enormous expectations across the continent. This is the context of *The Real Life of Alejandro Mayta*.

RG: Can we place the failed rebellion of Jauja within the wider context of guerrillas in Latin America?

MVLL: Yes: this story of the plot organized by Mayta and Lieutenant Vallejos happened all over Latin America. The Cuban experience showed that revolution could be created of its own initiative, instead of waiting—as the Communist Party proposed—for the objective conditions to arise. Che Guevara spread the message that when the conditions don't exist, you create them. And how do you create them? Going into the mountains, putting together a guerrilla group. The bases for the revolution can be immediately produced that way: there will come brutal repression by the army and the police, with torture and murder, that will stoke society's indignation, and there will be peasants, workers, students, and intellectuals participating in the armed struggle. Cuba is the proof that this is not just theory: it is an action plan that produces concrete results.

The reality is more complicated because the Cuban Revolution was not just made by the bearded ones in the Sierra Maestra: it was a movement that had international support, of a variety of sectors that applauded those young people who had risen up against the bloody dictator that was

Batista. Even the United States supported the movement: Herbert Matthews, a *New York Times* reporter who traveled to the Sierra Maestra, published a series of articles presenting Fidel Castro and his men as romantic guerrillas in search of freedom and justice for their country. This helped them a lot. In addition, in the United States, drives were organized to buy weapons and send them to those young people.

This proof that the revolution could take off with a very determined vanguard group encouraged the creation of guerrilla movements in all of Latin America. Today, we see that things did not happen as Che Guevara imagined them. Instead of a multiplication of revolutions, the opposite took place: soldiers mobilized, they squashed guerrilla movements, and they established more brutal and repressive dictatorships than prior regimes. Even a country with a tradition of democracy such as Uruguay imposed a military dictatorship as a response to the Tupamaros guerrillas. In Chile, another country with a tradition of democracy, the army delivered a coup d'état to oust the government of Salvador Allende and created a brutal dictatorship. Overall, the only thing the guerrilla movements did was to make Latin America go even further backward, destroying democracies that were imperfect and turning them into repressive, brutal, and corrupt military regimes. This is the context of the novel.

MIGUEL CABALLERO-VÁZQUEZ: Continuing with the theme of historical context: there is a parallel between *The Real Life of Alejandro Mayta* and *Conversation in The Cathedral*. The latter is a work written in the sixties about the failed revolutions in the fifties, and *Mayta* is a book published in the eighties that relays a failed revolutionary in the sixties.

MVLL: *Conversation in The Cathedral* narrates a world prior to the Cuban Revolution, when there still wasn't a case of a triumphant revolution.

ALEXANDRA APARICIO: The political situation that appears in the novel is more violent than what Peru's really was in the sixties.

MVLL: Exactly: the Peru of *The Real Life of Alejandro Mayta* is practically a country out of science fiction because it is invaded, it is occupied.

AA: And it seems that there are certain parallels between the apocalyptic context of *The Real Life of Alejandro Mayta* and the violence that Peru experienced later, in the eighties.

MVLL: The research the narrator does is not simply gratuitous: it is an effort to understand the present of a country at war. Old enemies—the right and the left, the capitalists and the revolutionaries—are destroying Peru. So what the narrator is searching for in his interviews is also a response to those great questions of the present: Now what? What is the correct position? Where does good lie and where does evil lie? That reality of violence and civil war already potentially existed at the time of Mayta's failed uprising, but it didn't activate until many years later.

This relationship between the situation of Peru in 1984 and the reality narrated in *The Real Life of Alejandro Mayta* is very important. In the book, there is an apocalyptic present, a present that never existed in reality, that is pure fantasy: one of an entire continent completely fractured by war.

RG: Could we summarize the novel as a critique of radicalism? Of the most radical left's politics?

MVLL: Peru had the experience of extreme radicalism with the war that unleashed the Sendero Luminoso (Shining Path) and that had terrible consequences: it left almost sixty thousand dead, thousands of towns upended, homes destroyed, and families severed. The peasants, who already had abominable living conditions, fell into even worse misery. That radicalism was an absolute failure that aggravated Peru's problems.

There is also a critical or intellectual radicalism that has offered a great service to Peru, denouncing horrors, corruption, and the country's and Latin America's great mistakes. Ours is a country with great resources that could have a very high standard of living but it has wasted them. This intellectual radicalism is very beneficial for the country and for the progress of any society. It has to do with a thinking that goes to the extreme to denounce lies and to try to find a truth that is elusive. That radicalism can manifest itself in philosophy, in thought, in literature, in the arts.

LITERARY TECHNIQUE

RG: In *The Real Life of Alejandro Mayta*, as in almost all of your novels, there is a very conscious decision not to include dates or concrete details that allow one to place what is narrated in an exact year. The narrator goes along dropping clues that are more or less hidden about the time period, numbers that a witty reader can start adding up, subtracting, until they get to the point of calculating a character's age or the years that have passed between one episode and another. Can you talk to us about that decision?

MVLL: I don't know where it comes from, but I have always tried to avoid dates in my novels when I can. I prefer to leave the reader with a certain ambiguity. But I don't know why. I don't have an answer. It doesn't follow any formal principle, although it is a constant in my work.

RG: But in your novels, time is always worked out in arithmetic terms. When a reader starts to add and subtract, a perfect chronology appears. Obviously, you as a writer have an outline in which the dates are very clear.

MVLL: Yes, but that outline starts getting fuzzy in the process of narration.

RG: Jennifer Shyue wrote something very interesting about the multiplicity of narrative voices in the novel. She tells us, "We can think there are 4.5 Maytas and 3.5 narrators because the borders between Mayta and the narrator blur in many parts of the novel."

JENNIFER SHYUE: Yes, at the beginning of the novel, there is synchrony between the narrative voice and Mayta's point of view. But in the final chapter, everything changes and the reader discovers that Mayta is the invention of an invented narrator.

MVLL: Exactly. It is a superposition of stories that in the end turns out to be just one. The variety of stories that are superimposed, that correct each other, that complement or reject each other, in the end create one sole story made of diversities, of complexities, of contradictions. Perhaps, in the end, all lives are like that. When we try to reconstruct a life, we discover that there are incoherencies and paradoxes, and that the testimonies we can gather are always very subjective—many times, they tell us more about the writer. Save for very exceptional cases, there is never absolute coherence.

JS: Why do you sometimes change the narrative voice to third person?

MVLL: Because within the narrator's voice, the voices of the characters themselves speak. This is a technique that is very present in the modern novel. There is a narrative voice, but different voices emerge from within that same voice, each with its own personality. Then the narrator's voice absorbs them again, so that the reader is left with just one voice. It is a technique that Faulkner uses in his novels. It's a very nice contrast because it generates great insecurity in the world the reader is getting to know: everything seems less clear, narrated by all those intermingled subjectivities. We see it, for example, in *As I Lay Dying*, which continues to seem to me to be one of Faulkner's best novels, and which tells the story of a family who takes the corpse of one of its members to be buried somewhere else. The family members are traveling along with that decaying corpse, and only the characters' minds speak, presenting a succession of consciousnesses in motion. Those consciousnesses, which are very different— there is, for example, a mentally deficient one—make up a very contradictory and complex story. I was fascinated by that novel and perhaps *Mayta*'s construction owes something to my recollection of its structure.

THE CHARACTERS

The Narrator

RG: Could you talk to us about the narrator of *The Real Life of Alejandro Mayta*, who is also a character in the novel?

MVLL: The narrator is always a character, in all novels. He can be visible or invisible, but the narrator is the main character of every novel. There is someone who tells what happened, and that someone is never the author, but rather a voice that the author invents. The author becomes impersonal and invents a character who narrates. It can be a narrator-character, an omniscient narrator, but it is always an invented narrator.

RG: The narrator of *The Real Life of Alejandro Mayta* is very different from the other characters in the novel and, at the end of the day, is very much like Mario Vargas Llosa.

MVLL: He is a narrator who wants to write Mayta's story and who relays how he went about writing this novel, gathering testimonies, looking at documents, adding a bit of imagination to them, adding his own personality into the book. He is an invisible narrator, but at the same time he is visible because of his works.

RG: The narrator of *The Real Life of Alejandro Mayta* has no name. No one calls him by his name, but people recognize him as a famous Peruvian writer, with international renown. Could you talk a little bit about the decision to make this character-narrator a kind of alter ego?

MVLL: That narrator came about in a very natural way. I started writing, as I always do with my novels: as I did my research, I would write not only notes but also small scenes. And it turned out that the person who narrated was implied in the story. Many times, the way I would collect those testimonies showed how the characters were connected, or whether they were close or distant witnesses of what had happened with Mayta. It was very important that whoever brought together those testimonies classify them, comparing and considering them against other statements. That started giving the narrator a central role that finally made him move around in the plot like one more character. But this happened along the way: I never conceived of it thus beforehand, nor did I want the narrator to be the one who told the story. It was the story itself that went about making him and giving him certain characteristics.

Mayta

RG: Mayta is a revolutionary, but he is also someone marginalized by the society in which he lives: he is poor; he has no family and no career.

MVLL: This is an important aspect. I realized that Mayta was the embodiment of the marginal: he had spent his entire life on the margins and was never part of that central current that consists of existing within society. He was a communist, an APRA-ist, a militant in parties that placed him underground.

At a given moment, I thought of making him homosexual. I said to myself, "It would be an even more radical way of demonstrating his absolute marginalization." At the time in which the story is set—the 1960s—the left, particularly the communist left, was deeply homophobic.

Carlos Franqui—who was the editor of *Revolución*, the newspaper that Fidel Castro put out there in the Sierra and that later became the official newspaper—says that in early meetings of the Council of Ministers, the revolutionaries asked each other, "What do we do with homosexuals? How should the Cuban Revolution treat homosexuality?" They discussed the matter at length until the Cuban leadership consulted other socialist countries, the Soviet Union, China, the republics of Eastern Europe. Of all the responses, the Chinese one was the most hair-raising, as the Chinese stated they had solved that problem by executing all the homosexuals. Cuba wavered in its policy on this subject until the mid-1960s, when the revolution organized raids on homosexuals and then sent them to UMAP camps.

The first time I seriously questioned the Cuban Revolution was when I learned of the UMAP camps. I knew a group of young people—many of them homosexuals and lesbians—who made up a movement called El Puente. They supported the revolution and thought that the new regime would foment an open and tolerant atmosphere in the sexual arena. Suddenly, they were jailed and sent to concentration camps. Many intellectuals around the world, who until then had unconditionally supported the Revolution, protested against Fidel Castro's government.

I wanted to make Mayta homosexual to imagine the conflicts his identity would cause with his own comrades. When the book came out, the strongest attacks—and I think that

The Real Life of Alejandro Mayta is the book of mine that has spurred the most violent criticism—came from groups on the left, who were terribly homophobic at the time. I recall one critic who claimed, "The caricature he makes of a revolutionary militant is so outrageous that he even presents him as a homosexual." As if being homosexual were so utterly despicable. Those articles prove the extent to which homophobia and sexual prejudice were deeply rooted in the Latin American left. On that matter, the left was as prejudiced as the right.

RG: The theme of sexuality is very present in all of your novels, from *The Time of the Hero* to *The Neighborhood*. In one way or another, sexuality on the margins—and in many cases, the darkest aspects of sexuality—appears in almost all of your books. There seems to be a great curiosity to understand how a whole series of eccentric or marginal sexual behaviors manifests itself in Latin American societies.

MVLL: It is a subject that is always there, hovering over people's sex lives. I grew up in a world in which homosexuals were deeply disdained and forced to lead secret lives, like in a catacomb. There were all kinds of twisted fantasies about them. When I was a boy, the greatest insult you could call another boy was *maricón*. That has changed, and today it is difficult to imagine the world of prejudices and lies that reigned in the 1950s. In those years, when I was active in the Communist Party, it was a subject you couldn't mention. Communists and priests had practically the same rigid position: both groups viewed homosexuality as an extreme aberration, as degeneracy.

There was, for example, a grotesque theory that came

from the Soviet Union, which we discussed one time in my Cahuide group cell. Ivan Pavlov argued that since there were no homosexuals in the countryside, homosexuality was urban degeneracy, a vice created by the decadent bourgeoisie. So, according to Pavlov, the best cure was to send homosexuals to work in the countryside, surrounded by healthy and hetero-sexual peasants. If they milked cows, he thought, they would cease to be homosexuals. Today, that seems funny, but that was the official policy of the Soviet Union, which Cuba later adopted in the 1960s.

MCV: There is a link between the characters of Mayta and Santiago Zavala, although they belong to completely differ-ent social classes. Santiago Zavala is the one who, when it comes down to it, doesn't dare to be a revolutionary: he goes in and out of the movement. What kind of character would Mayta have been in *Conversation in The Cathedral*?

MVLL: Mayta is a very poor guy, from a lower-middle-class family, bordering on working class. This is the world in which he is brought up, where he is educated. He goes to an ex-tremely poor school. But he doesn't belong to the same social class as Ambrosio, who comes from an even poorer world.

MCV: Could we imagine Mayta at the Universidad de San Marcos?

MVLL: Yes: Mayta would have gone to San Marcos, a univer-sity where kids of his social class studied.

MCV: Are they of the same generation?

MVLL: Mayta is much older than Santiago Zavala. Santiago is my age: in other words, he was much younger, as a character in *Conversation*, than the Mayta of the insurrection. Mayta is already an old man when he throws himself into that revolutionary adventure. That is the big difference between him and Francisco Vallejos, who is a twenty-two- or twenty-three-year-old guy at the time of the insurrection. Mayta's age is never given, but he's an old man; he's no longer made for revolutions, and that's what's interesting about the story, that he becomes young again thanks to Vallejos. Vallejos's spirit of adventure is contagious; it's something Mayta never had during his political trajectory.

The novel started from that idea: the old, experienced revolutionary who wants to instruct that young man and ends up himself under the tutelage of the young man, who infects him with his passion for adventure, for guerrilla struggles, and for military action. That subject gets a bit fuzzy because in the end, the novel narrates the story of the making of a Mayta.

CHARLOTTE WILLIAMS: In the novel, there are testimonies that present Mayta as a martyr and use practically religious terms to talk about him.

MVLL: Mayta was a great believer as a child and received a religious education. It's a very common occurrence: those who have been big believers and leave religion need to keep on believing, so they seek out a different dogma that they embrace with nearly religious fervor. In addition, Marxist ideology, just like religion, offers answers to everything because it is a self-sufficient mechanism. Popper observed that ideologies are irrefutable because they constitute a closed circuit that also requires complete faith.

I recently read *Diálogo de conversos* (A dialogue between two converts), a book written by two Chileans—Roberto Ampuero and Mauricio Rojas—who were communists and were miraculously saved during Pinochet's coup. They lived in exile and changed over time, turning into liberals. Roberto Ampuero had been a member of the Communist Party of Chile, while Mauricio Rojas was actively militant in the MIR [Movimiento de Izquierda Revolucionaria], which was even more radical. After the coup, Ampuero exiled himself in East Germany, where he married a Cuban woman who ended up being the daughter of one of the leaders of the revolution, General Fernando Flores Ibarra. They took him to Cuba, and there he began to discover the truth about socialism. He was left absolutely horrified by what he saw and by what he lived. In addition, since he was married to the daughter of one of the leaders, he could see what was happening from the inside. He wrote a fascinating, very sarcastic novel about those years in Havana: *Nuestros años verde olivo* (Our olive-green years). The left boycotted it, but despite that, it has been in circulation and continues to be. It is an indispensable book for understanding what happened in those years in Cuba.

Mauricio Rojas was even more radical: he was a member of the MIR, which sought armed revolution, and he came to commit acts of violence in Chile. After the coup, he spent his exile in Sweden, where he continued his links with the MIR. But in those years, he also devoted himself to studying: he learned Swedish, studied for a degree in economics, and realized, little by little, what an absurdity the ideological fantasy that the MIR represented was. He ended up turning into a liberal, like Roberto Ampuero. But in addition, he became a member of the Swedish Liberal Party and became a deputy. He has a great political career—which is remarkable in a culture so different from his own—and he defends the immigrant cause. He is a brilliant guy who has written with great eloquence about the cases of Cuba, Argentina, and Nicaragua.

So these two writers, who didn't know each other, get together to tell their stories in a dialogue. It is a book that reads like an adventure novel narrating the evolution they've experienced since their youth, in those years of Chile's Unidad Popular. There we find portrayed that Latin America dominated by intellectuals and leftist militants, where Mayta's story takes place.

Lituma

CW: In *The Real Life of Alejandro Mayta*, Sergeant Lituma appears, the same character we will later see in *Death in the Andes* and in other books. Why does he recur in so many of your novels?

MVLL: Sergeant Lituma and Lieutenant Silva recur in several stories. I don't know why. Lituma is a character who starts appearing in the first things I wrote. Whenever I begin a story, he shows up, offering his services. It's a curious thing, but I wouldn't be able to explain why. In addition, he is a run-of-the-mill character: a poor civil guard officer without any trace of greatness, who is good deep down, because he is moved by a sense of justice. He comes back constantly and has appeared in several stories—something that doesn't happen to me with other characters. The only thing I can say is that there's a certain affection with this Lituma.

CW: Is the character based on someone?

MVLL: Not that I can recall. A girl at San Marcos who wrote a thesis about my work surprised me with the discovery of an article that—she says—I wrote when I was in my last year at school in Piura. I didn't remember it—in fact, I still don't remember it and I've never managed to find it—but she says it appeared in *La Industria* and it shows that I wrote about a civil guard officer who was in charge of the Piura prefecture and who seemed a lot like Lituma. My grandfather was prefect of Piura, and I lived in the prefecture between the ages of ten and eleven. And it seems that in the article, I talk about how I became friends with that guard and I portray him singing to win the love of one of the prefecture's employees. He sang her songs of the period, such as "Muñequita linda," and he had a very beautiful voice. That article ended with the sentence "I think his name was Lituma," and the author of the thesis opined that the Lituma of my novels comes from there. But all of this I learned by reading the thesis, and then I said to myself, "So there was a Lituma in reality."

JS: So should the reader interpret the different Litumas who appear in your novels as the same character? Or are we dealing with different characters?

MVLL: I think that the character of Lituma is more or less the same one who appears in different stories: he is a civil guard officer, a very modest man with a certain sense of justice. There is something that pushes him in the direction of good most of the time. He is a man who has been in the jungle and who, in his youth, was a great party animal, a layabout: he liked to play guitar, to go dancing at the *chicherías*. One day, he plays Russian roulette at a brothel and a landowner ends up dead, so he ends up in jail. Then he becomes a civil guard, is sent to different parts of Peru and lives the adventure I tell in *Death in the Andes*. From there, he is sent to the jungle, where he lives the experience of *The Green House* before returning to Piura, where he has other adventures. We see him at the end of *The Green House* and also in *The Discreet Hero*, one of my last novels where he appears. The character's trajectory is more or less coherent, and his personality is more or less the same. He is a good guy, although he can commit many atrocities and many excesses, but his vocation is to be good deep down.

RG: You've never thought of writing a novel about Lituma that would bring together all of his experiences?

MVLL: Only about Lituma? No, it hasn't occurred to me. But I wouldn't rule out having him continue to appear in my novels, even though he isn't in *The Neighborhood*, the last one I published. I don't think that I would ever write a novel entirely about Lituma, because he is a secondary character, a routine, minor character, a person who can go unnoticed on the streets or in life, of the kind Flaubert calls "one of those human beings who is like a bridge because you cross them and then go elsewhere." It's a terrible image, that of character-bridge. He's good for crossing a small creek, and then you leave him behind without ever looking back.

JAUJA: THE SITE OF THE REBELLION

LARA NORGAARD: When Mayta arrives in Jauja for the first time, he describes this place as the cradle of the Peruvian Revolution. At other times, it is associated with gold or with tuberculosis. Can you talk to us about how you incorporated the mythology of Jauja in the novel?

MVLL: In the nineteenth century, it was believed that the climate of Jauja was propitious for curing tuberculosis. Many people with tuberculosis were sent to Jauja, and you can still see the building today that housed the hospital that received thousands of the sick, rich and poor, from all over Peru. That made for many jokes about Jauja as the city of tuberculosis victims. With time came the discovery that that was a fantasy and that Jauja's climate wasn't particularly good. And before that, during the colonial era, Jauja was associated with mines: that is where Peru's gold came from.

LN: The novel presents tuberculosis as a myth, as an illness mythologized by literature and romantic sensibilities.

MVLL: Exactly. There are many novels written in the nineteenth century, during the romantic and modernist period, that take place in Jauja and deal with the subject of tuberculosis. The authors were imitating Thomas Mann: they wanted to write Peruvian versions of *The Magic Mountain* and imagined Jauja as the Latin American equivalent of Davos, the Swiss city where those with tuberculosis ended up. An example would be *La ciudad de los tísicos* (The city of the consumptives), a novel by Abraham Valdelomar.

As a young man, I worked at a newspaper, and one day I was talking to the director, whose name was Pedro del Pino Fajardo, and he told me that when he was a boy he had had tuberculosis and been sent to the hospital in Jauja. That experience left such a mark on him that he later published a novel, *Sanatorio al desnudo* (The naked sanatorium), in which he presents a very eccentric theory about the Koch bacillus.

JS: Jauja is the site of a rebellion, but it also represents, to the narrator, a certain peace and tranquility. At the end of chapter 9, this image appears:

> When I go to sleep, I hear, at last, a rhythmic noise. No, they are not nocturnal birds; it's the wind, which slaps the waters of the Paca laguna against the residence's terrace. That soft music and the beautiful starred Jauja night sky suggest a peaceful country, of satisfied and lucky people. They lie, just like fiction.

MVLL: Paca is a lake on the outskirts of Jauja. When I went to Jauja to interview its residents and ask them what they recalled about the insurrection, the extraordinary beauty of that lake up high made an impression on me. There was a full moon, and that landscape suggested an absolutely peaceful world, calm, happy, an image that was the exact opposite of what the history of that place contained, so marked by violence, blood, repression, isolation, poverty. Jauja is an extremely poor city. It is a great irony that the city was once a symbol of riches, because although it is surrounded by former gold mines, what you see on the streets is terrible poverty.

THE END

RG: The last chapter of *The Real Life of Alejandro Mayta* puts to the test everything that has been presented in the rest of the novel. The reader has certain ideas about who Mayta was, about what happened, and suddenly realizes that all of this information could be false.

MVLL: When Mayta appears, reality bursts into the story. He offers an unexpected presence and gives a testimony that is the final turn of the screw.

RG: As a matter of fact, Mayta's homosexuality, which seems practically confirmed in all the interviews, is left unproven. The Mayta who appears in that final chapter is rather homophobic.

MVLL: He is a character who has every prejudice in the world. The last chapter is a commentary on the border between reality and fiction. The previous chapters contained a lot of fiction: the narrator invents, adds, and fills in gaps with imagination, and in the end reality corrects him. The definitive result unfurls the ingredients of fiction: we see the ingredients mingling, rejecting each other, or complementing each other.

JS: In addition to adding the last chapter, in which the meeting with Mayta is told, did you make changes to the previous sections after your meeting with the real Mayta?

MVLL: When I wrote the last chapter, the novel was practically finished. Of course, I made some corrections to avoid contradictions that were too flagrant, but I had already finished writing and the book could have finished there, at chapter 9, if I had not discovered that Mayta's model was alive.

It seemed important to me to include the interview, something that added to the novel's reality. I thought, "Here's Mayta. Talk to him, and you're going to realize that he's another character."

I've experienced each of the novels I've written as an adventure. As I researched, very rich materials would come up. That is why, when I begin a novel, I really like to begin the research, because things are going to start coming up that really enrich the initial project.

HOW THE NOVEL WAS RECEIVED

DIEGO NEGRÓN-REICHARD: In the prologue, you confirm that this novel was the most poorly received of all your books. How do you explain the hostility shown by critics? Why was that abuse aimed at this work and not others?

MVLL: I think the novel was abused because at the time—the mid-1980s—the left still wouldn't accept criticism. Today, it is still very defensive, but at least we can say that it has done its own self-criticism and has become more tolerant. In those years, the left was as if frozen in its ideological truths such that it couldn't be moved: a dogmatic mechanism that aimed to explain it all, give answers to everything, and never admit its own mistakes. When *Mayta* came out—with its portrait of a left that fools itself as a result of ideological fantasies, that cannot accept reality—it caused tremendous irritation.

Even so, as I have said, perhaps the fact that spurred the

most ferocious criticism was that Mayta seemed homosexual. I say "seemed" because in the end we discover that he is not homosexual, that that is simply one of the many versions in circulation among the testimonies. But the mere insinuation that a revolutionary could be homosexual was very scandalous.

RG: So the most critical reactions to the novel happened primarily in Peru?

MVLL: All over, there were very tough criticisms. Not just in Latin America but also in Spain. And they came, above all, from a homophobic and intolerant left.

RG: And did that also happen with the translations?

MVLL: The critics were more tolerant in other languages, but in the Spanish-speaking world there was a lot of hostility. It is a novel that has been the object of ideological controversies. I always remained curious about whether the real Mayta ever read it.

RACE

MARLIS HINCKLEY: In *The Real Life of Alejandro Mayta*, like in other novels, race is of great importance: it's specific about who is white, who is *cholo*, especially when the narrator tries to reconstruct the insurrection.

MVLL: In Peru—and in the majority of Latin American countries—race is a hushed subject that isn't out in the open but that is always present in people's behaviors. Our countries are deeply racist, in all directions. Not only because whites consider themselves superior to Blacks and Indians and *cholos*, but because Blacks consider themselves superior to mestizos, and Indians superior to Blacks. Prejudices go from top to bottom and from bottom to top. At the same time, it's very covered up, because official policies insist there is no racism, that we are all equal. Economic factors also affect the definition of who is Indian, who is Black, *cholo*, or white. Of "white whites," there are very few in Peru: they are an insignificant minority. There are people who consider themselves white, because someone who has money is whiter than someone who doesn't. Money whitens people, and poverty makes them more *cholo*. If you're poor and live like a poor person, then you cease to be white; you become less and less white and become a *cholo*, a mestizo, a little Indian. A rich Black person is almost white. Prejudice covers not only race but also money. A *cholo* with money is already white and is no longer treated like a *cholo*. At the same time, there is a revindication of race, for example, the regionalist trends. In the 1930s, there was a *cholist* trend in Peruvian literature: novels and stories that told the lives of *cholos*, and that presented the *cholo* as the essence of Peru. Because *cholos* had invented creole music, dances, creole food—in other words, everything that defines Peruvian culture.

But everything related to race is very subtle and rarely comes out into the open. You see, for example, when there's a fight and someone insults his opponent as a "shitty *cholo*" or "*blanquito*," "*blanquiñoso*." That configuration is very present in people's lives and appears in their vocabulary, but nobody officially recognizes it because the country is not supposed to be racist. All Latin American countries and perhaps all countries in general are racist. In all of them, there are racial prejudices that make it so certain people feel superior because of the color of their skin. In my novels, this phenomenon always appears. This is a constant.

Fortunately, we've been evolving, not just in Peru but in all of Latin America. Today, racism is much less extensive than twenty or thirty years ago. It is still there, but to a much lesser degree. And political polarization, which was so ferocious when I was younger, has softened considerably because there is a practice of democratic coexistence. I think that is true of Latin America as a whole, in general. There is true progress that is very far from ideal but that we have to take into account. If we judge Latin America by virtue of what it was forty years ago, we have made a lot of progress on all fronts. Now, if we judge it by virtue of the ideal, of course it still has many defects today. But what is not in doubt is that the Latin America of my childhood has evolved dramatically into the Latin America of today. We have made gigantic steps.

IDEOLOGICAL PURITANISM

VICTORIA NAVARRO: Vallejos meets Mayta at a party where everyone is dancing, except Mayta, because he doesn't like to dance. The interesting thing is that Mayta doesn't want Vallejos to realize he has no sense of rhythm, as if that could discredit him.

MVLL: Mayta is very puritanical: he is against dancing and against fun in general. He is a kind of revolutionary I have met who is like a priest, handing himself over body and soul to militancy and not allowing any type of relaxation because that, in some way, would be betraying the cause. It is a religious attitude: that of creating a different world, a paradise on earth.

RG: We could say the same of Fidel Castro.

MVLL: Fidel Castro is the type of revolutionary who always speaks of the future, of a world of equality, of fraternity, of true freedom. Ultimately, that utopia is not so different from the one Saint Augustine presents in *The City of God*.

RG: And Fidel Castro didn't dance, either.

MVLL: Neither did Lenin. Who can imagine Lenin dancing?

RG: The novel also plays with form and with the conventions of journalistic chronicles. It is practically a parody of that genre, as if a journalist had done his research but in the end the story's protagonist has the power to edit him, to impose his version of events.

MVLL: Much more than a story, the novel narrates the construction of a story, the way it starts coming together through researching reality, with a lot of support from fantasy, imagination.

MH: There is a moment in which Senator Campos tells the narrator that he is going to speak very frankly because he's dealing with a work of fiction, although when it comes down to it, perhaps he is not as frank as he says. I wanted to ask you if in real life you had the same experience: Did people seem to act more open with you because you were writing fiction instead of a report?

MVLL: That's a good question. I think so, that in general people spoke to me with more freedom, thinking that I wasn't going to use their testimony for a journalistic chronicle, where truth is supposed to matter very much, but rather for fiction. But what made the greatest impression on me was that people, during the interviews, tried to justify themselves a posteriori. Some would say, "The act of going with four people to a hill to shoot any which way was an absurdity and an act of suicide," despite everything indicating that they had supported the uprising. Others had been friends and accomplices of Mayta's but now accused him of being a CIA agent. I realized that the testimony they were giving was contaminated by later history, by the way in which the revolution had failed.

MELANCHOLY

KYLE BERLIN: In *The Real Life of Alejandro Mayta*, as in the majority of your novels, the characters suffer a great melancholy. Where does this sadness come from?

MVLL: That's a good observation. There is a basic melancholy in the experiences that are the raw material of my novels. Like all novelists, I work from memory, because that is where images are kept that go on to be the starting point of a story. During the work process, it is impossible for nostalgia not to arise, a somewhat melancholic vision of the years of my youth, the years I'm evoking as I'm imagining a story set in that time period. That melancholy is the emotional context of the stories told, especially the ones that are based on events of the past. These are eras that I, in some way, have lived, although not in the exact way as these characters, but the context corresponds to what I lived. To my chagrin, writing can be impregnated with a lot of nostalgia for a lost childhood, for adolescence, for the years of my youth that mark my personality.

ENDING NOTE

RG: Could you comment on the novel's last sentence? "And I'll remember that a year ago I began to concoct this story the same way I'm ending it, by speaking about the garbage that's invading every neighborhood in the capital of Peru."

MVLL: *The Real Life of Alejandro Mayta* begins and ends with the same vision of the trash dumps. It's a pessimistic ending because the book has not been able to distance itself from that trash that invades everything.

5

WHO KILLED PALOMINO MOLERO?

Who Killed Palomino Molero? (1986) begins when a tortured corpse is discovered, setting off an extensive investigation. Sergeant Lituma and Lieutenant Silva interview all of the local inhabitants, including Colonel Mindreau, a powerful soldier in the region who becomes one of the main suspects and who ends up killing himself before the crime can be solved. How to establish the truth is one of the main questions posed by the novel.

RUBÉN GALLO: Just like *The Real Life of Alejandro Mayta*, *Who Killed Palomino Molero?* is a novel based on a real event, on minor news that occurred in Peru and that you researched in order to write fiction.

MARIO VARGAS LLOSA: Yes, the story I tell in *Who Killed Palomino Molero?* is real. It's based on the disappearance of a young military aviation soldier who was apparently a run-of-the-mill guy, nothing remarkable, who didn't stand out in any way. One day they found him dead, and it turned out he had been abused before being killed. There was an investigation, and when someone said they'd seen the little soldier with the daughter of the air base's director, the case was immediately covered up.

At that time, Peru still lived under the Odría dictatorship and soldiers were untouchable. Everyone thought that the kid was courting the daughter of the military base's director and that he was then punished and killed. The investigation was never finished, it was interrupted and buried, but a rumor was left floating in the air and there were many questions: What happened? Did they bury that story because it implicated soldiers? That's what one is given to understand in my novel.

The real story took place in Talara, a very small coastal city in the Piura region, which I visited in 1946 and again in 1952. It was very well known because it contained a U.S.-Canadian company that exploited petroleum resources and also an air base, which is where the kid's disappearance happens. The story I tell is invented on the basis of that sole detail, the discovery of the corpse of a young soldier who has been ferociously abused.

The novel has the structure of a detective story. I wanted to create deliberate suspense around that death, and there Lituma reappears, that character who turns up every time I start a story, volunteering himself for the plot. It's as if he were saying to me, "No, you haven't used me enough. You've wasted me until now in the stories you've told. I'm still here, I can continue to be of value to you." Of all the characters I've created, he is the one who reappears most in my stories, and I still don't know how to explain why.

Palomino Molero was going to be a short story but ended up being a novella. Something similar happened to me with *Captain Pantoja and the Special Service*: I started writing a story I wanted to be brief, but I began feeling more and more pressure to extend it, to expand it, to link it to other stories. It's a tendency I always have as I begin writing: although my initial idea is of a very clean, clear story, it starts getting tangled up little by little. It's a kind of natural vocation toward a labyrinth, toward entanglement, toward complexity, so that the story gains greater intensity, greater depth, a dimension that goes beyond pure anecdote.

PIURA

RG: *Who Killed Palomino Molero?* is also set in the region of Piura, a city that appears in several of your novels and also in your memoir. Can you talk to us about the importance of that place in your work?

MVLL: My relationship with Piura, that city in the north of Peru, close to the border with Ecuador, is very important. Curiously, it has left quite a mark on me: I lived in Piura for only two years, which weren't even entire years, but school years. I arrived when I was ten or eleven and studied fifth grade there, in the Salesian Fathers school, and later the last year of elementary school in San Miguel de Piura, at a state school. I spent just a few months there, and nevertheless I have written so much about that city: my novels *The Green House* and *The Discreet Hero* are set there; as are at least three of the five tales in *The Cubs and Other Stories*, my first book of stories; and the play *La Chunga*.

Piura left a great mark on me, and I couldn't explain why. The same thing happened with a two-week trip I made to the Amazon in the year 1958, but that made such an impression on me that I wrote three books inspired by that experience.

Piura left an enormous number of images in my memory that have later been starting points for stories.

Why Piura? Perhaps because my first memories of Peru take place there. Although I was born in Arequipa, my family moved with me when I was a year old—I have no memories of the city in which I was born—and I spent my entire childhood in Bolivia. As happens with expatriate families, mine lived with great nostalgia and dreamed of returning to Peru. I grew up with that longing and, when I could, the first city I lived in was Piura. The landscape, which contrasted so much with the Andean sierra of Cochabamba, made quite an impression on me. Piura was surrounded by deserts, and sand rained down on the houses. It was a very small city, and from the corners you could see the desert, and the landscape changed as the wind broke down and remade the sand dunes.

I arrived in Piura when I was ten years old and recall that my classmates mocked my accent because I spoke like a Bolivian, like a *serranito*, a kid from the highlands. They would bother me, saying "sh, sh, sh," because people from the highlands pronounce "s" like "sh." "*Sherrano*, you're a *sherrano*," they would say to me, mocking my way of speaking. I would ask my mother, "If I'm Peruvian, why do they make fun of me?" They made me feel like a foreigner, and that was very painful to me.

Piura was also linked to a certain age of innocence. Until the age of ten, I was completely naïve about sexual matters, something that at the time was very common in Peru and in Bolivia, in contrast to today, when ten-year-old kids already know everything. At that age I still believed, although it seems like a joke, that storks brought babies from Paris. And I imagine that not just me, but many kids my age, all over Latin America, believed the same because what reigned in education was a very conservative attitude that was very closed-minded about sexual matters.

I remember that one afternoon I had gone to bathe in the river with some classmates from school. They started talking, and little by little I discovered that it wasn't true that storks brought babies from Paris. I learned, by listening to my friends, how things happened in reality. For me, it was a real trauma to think that I had been born like that. I thought, "How terrible, how dirty! That's what sex is? How disgusting! What a nasty thing!" It caused me real trauma that lasted for a long time. Perhaps it is because of that traumatic revelation that the memories of Piura persist with such vividness in my memory and have enriched my work as a writer. Later, I started getting used to the idea and it started seeming less and less repugnant, until I realized that there was a certain humor about it.

Now that I am old, there are still images of Piura that come up and push me to fantasize about that place, and I won't rule out writing other stories set there in the future, although it would be a place that no longer exists, because the city I have in my memory—small, surrounded by deserts— has ceased to exist today. The desert has been transformed into small irrigated farms, and now the landscape is green. In fact, it is one of the Peruvian cities that has seen the most progress in recent years. In my novel *The Discreet Hero*, it already appears as a very different city.

LANGUAGE

RG: Could you talk to us about the use of regionalisms in the novel?

MVLL: The Piuran way of speaking is very different: the singsonginess, the musicality of the accent is immediately recognizable, although modernization has erased those regional variations. But when I was a boy, the Piuran way of speaking was very marked. I have never wanted to make picturesque literature, to write tales that were too focused on a certain way of speaking, because I think the exploitation of local color did a lot of damage to Latin American literature at one time. But in *Palomino*, that musicality of Piuran speech really served me to create a prototypical environment of the place. That is why in that novel, as in *The Green House* and *The Discreet Hero*, there is a constant, but prudent, use of local speech.

What does "prudent" mean? I am referring to a functional use of language that allows the characters to express themselves in a way that marks them as inhabitants of a specific place and time. But it is very important that the way of speaking doesn't swallow up the character and turn into the tale's main ingredient, which is what happens in nativism, in Creoleism, and in picturesque literature that exploits local color. I don't want a tale to revolve around a certain way of speaking or of expressing oneself; I want the mode of expression to deepen the psychological characteristics, in the idiosyncrasy, in the behavior of my characters. So although I use many local mannerisms or, as in the first sentence, a very special musicality, I've always sought for the story and the character to be what is important, what is fundamental, and not the local color of what is spoken. That is the difference between realist literature and folkloric literature, in which folklore prevails over what is literary, as we've seen in certain periods of Peruvian literature and of Latin American literature.

RG: Could you talk to us about the word *jijunagrandísimas*, which is the novel's first word. The story opens with this surprising phrase:

> *Jijunagrandísimas*. Lituma felt the vomit rising in his throat.
> "Kid, they really did a job on you."
>   The boy had been both hung and impaled on the old carob tree. His position was so absurd that he looked more like a scarecrow or a broken marionette than a corpse.

MVLL: "*Jijunagrandísima*" is shorthand for *grandísimo hijo de puta*, or "that enormous son of a bitch." There's an *h* that becomes a *j* to give the expression greater power. With those two *j*'s, the word "*jijuna*" is very violent; it expresses power and vulgarity. It is also a euphemism that avoids mentioning the mother, although anyone who hears it and is in the know will recognize that "*jijunagrandísima*" is the worst insult one can pronounce.

RG: Why did you decide to start the narration with that word?

MVLL: For several reasons. First, I wanted to show that this story is happening in a working-class world, where this language frequently occurs. A more educated person would say "*hijo de puta*" and not "*jijunagrandísima*." A reader from Piura, a Peruvian reader, immediately understands that we're dealing with a very working-class context.

RG: Is that a typical Piuran expression?

MVLL: No, it is said all over Peru, or at least it was said when I was a boy. I remember that at school, no one said "*hijo de* *puta*" because it was a very violent expression, but rather "*ji-juna*," where the insult was softened by the euphemism. There's an apocope there, something silenced.

That bad word also foreshadows the terrible violence that will take place in the story.

LITERARY TECHNIQUE: HIDDEN DETAILS

RG: In this novel, you use a narrative technique that you have called "hidden details." There are basic elements of the plot—starting with the question posed by the title: Who killed Palomino Molero?—that are never resolved. The most important facts to explain what happened are absent from the story.

MVLL: Yes. Hemingway relayed that he discovered the secret to his art one day while he was writing a story that ended with the main character's suicide. He didn't know how to tell it, so he would rewrite it and rewrite it, until suddenly, it occurred to him to hide the story's main event, and not narrate the main character's suicide. He discovered that silence could be loquacious, could become a silence that would speak very loudly to the reader because it would leave him at the edge of a cliff, asking himself what really happened. That is why it is the reader who has to decide if the main character committed suicide or not. Hemingway's stories and novels play a lot with those silences, and that is why they hide so many things. "The Killers," for example, tells the story of two gunmen who arrive at a U.S. city and ask for a gentleman they don't know but whom they must kill because they are paid assassins. A friend finds out and runs to warn the gentleman, telling him, "Run, they're coming to kill you." But the man doesn't move and seems resigned to being killed. It is an example of how the most important thing is silenced: the reason for which this man does not run and accepts dying, being murdered. There's a film adaptation of this story—*The Killers*, directed by Don Siegel, in which Ronald Reagan plays a minor role—that is very nice because it is told from the point of view of one of the assassins, who thinks it all very strange after the murder because he says, "When a man is going to be killed—and I've killed many—that man reacts: he runs, he gets scared, he cries or fights. He goes out to face you. But someone who is waiting to be killed with such resignation, I've never seen that. There's something strange about this character we've killed." So the goon starts to research why his victim didn't react, and that leads him to reconstruct the life and identity of that person he didn't know. And the film gives another turn of the screw to the story, which isn't in Hemingway's writing: after finding out who his victim was, he goes to kill the bad guy who hired him and says to him, "I already know why that gentleman had no reaction. Because he was already dead. You killed him twenty years ago, with your monstrous betrayal, taking his woman away and pinning a crime on him that he didn't commit. He was already dead and I killed a dead man." It's very well done because the outline of Hemingway's story can be filled in a thousand different ways. He simply narrates the outline of a story that the reader must complete, participating very actively in bringing the tale to life.

Palomino Molero owes much to that idea. In my youth, I read Hemingway quite enthusiastically, especially his short stories. If there is any book of mine in which Hemingway's distant influence is felt, surely it is *Palomino Molero*. Not because of what it says, but because of what it doesn't: there are many silenced elements in that story.

THE CHARACTERS

Mindreau

RG: In *Palomino Molero* there is a character who reminds me of the Cayo Bermúdez of *Conversation*: Colonel Mindreau, one of the air base's soldiers, who is also a dark employee of the state who abuses the power conferred on him by his rank.

MVLL: He is a gruesome, ferocious, terrible character.

RG: But Mindreau is less terrible than Cayo Bermúdez and seems to redeem himself in the end. Although the end of the novel is ambiguous, one possible reading would end with Mindreau having a change of heart.

MVLL: There is ambiguity in the novel's closing. If Mindreau had been an incestuous murderer, the reader would not have accepted it. The reader's reaction is always protective: if a reader runs into an absolutely monstrous character, he feels contaminated by that monstrosity and his self-defense mechanism is not to believe, to say, "No, this is an exaggeration, this goes beyond the acceptable, and as such, this has nothing to do with me or with real human beings." You have to mock the reader's defenses so that the story can be accepted by him.

That is why the end of the novel is ambiguous and the reader asks himself what actually happened: Was it all an invention by the schizophrenic daughter who imagines things? Or perhaps Mindreau himself is the schizophrenic one, because he plays at having two personalities, one with his family and the other in public? That is something the reader has to decide. If I had given a sole, definitive solution, the story would run the risk of being judged unbelievable. The character would have ended up being so monstrous that the reader would reject him and, with him, the entire plot.

RG: The novel plays a lot with the idea of truth. What is truth and how can we establish it? At the end, many questions remain without clear answers, many ambiguities that the reader must resolve. Something that we do know with certainty is that Mindreau commits suicide by shooting himself.

MVLL: Yes: that suicide is a truth in the novel, as opposed to many other elements that are never clarified.

Doña Adriana

RG: Now I'd like to talk about a passage, nearly at the end of *Palomino Molero*, that narrates a very funny scene. Lieutenant Silva spends a large part of the novel wanting to woo Doña Adriana, the owner of the town's bar, but she doesn't pay him any mind. One day, he decides to go to this woman's house to force her to accept him. But she ends up being a very strong woman—much stronger than Silva or the reader could have imagined—and the one who ends up losing is Silva.

MVLL: Doña Adriana is a resourceful woman: she humiliates the lieutenant and leaves him frozen. She uses psychology to win the battle.

RG: It's a very complex scene. It's worth rereading the passage in which Doña Adriana narrates Silva's visit to Lituma. There we see how she manages to scare off the lieutenant using language as her only weapon. Doña Adriana recalls:

"[Silva] began by telling me a bunch of silly things . . . *I can't go on living this way. I'm drowning in my desire for you. This desire I feel is killing me, I've reached my limit. If I don't have you, I'll end up blowing my brains out. Or maybe I'll kill you . . .*

"I took off my nightgown and lay there naked . . . I said some things to your boss he never dreamed he'd hear. Filth." . . . *Here I am, why don't you strip, cholito. Doña Adriana went on, her voice vibrating with indignation. She thrust forward her breasts and her stomach and held her hands at her waist. Or are you ashamed to show it to me? Is it that small, daddy? Come on, hurry up, take off your pants and show it to me. Come on, take me right now. Show me what a man you really are, baby. Give it to me five times in a row, that's what my husband does every night. He's old and you're young, so you can break his record easily, right? Give it to me, six or seven times. Can you do it? . . . Go on, baby, take off your pants. Let me see your dick. I want to see how big it is and to count how many times you'll come. Think you'll reach eight?"*

". . . He was totally destroyed. You should have seen him . . ."

". . . Of course he didn't take off his pants or anything else. Whatever lust he had when he came in evaporated just like that."

I didn't come here to be made fun of, shouted the lieutenant, not knowing how he was going to get out.

"Of course not, you son of a bitch. You came here to scare me

with your gun and to rape me, so you could feel you were a real *man. Well, go ahead and rape me. Superman. Go on, get busy.* *Rape me ten times in a row, daddy. I'll be satisfied. What are* *you waiting for?"*

. . . "Yes, I did go crazy. But it worked. Your boss took off like a shot with his tail between his legs. And he made out that it was I who offended him, the wise guy!

. . . "Look at him now. No spirit left. I'm almost sorry for him."

MVLL: In the novel, the narration is interwoven: Doña Adriana speaks with Lituma in the present, but the tale of her encounter with Silva is in the past. This scene—grotesque, but also very funny—serves as a counterweight to the story of the murdered soldier, which is terrible. Doña Adriana's tale contains many bad words, but they are used with a lot of humor to decrease their vulgarity.

RG: There is a very entertaining moment in which, after the string of filthy things that Doña Adriana tells him, Silva responds, "You don't have the right to treat me this way," forgetting that he had come to rape her.

MVLL: Of course, Silva expected a passive attitude, by a scared woman, but the woman gains the high ground on him very quickly. The reader discovers that deep down, Silva isn't such a bad person: another man could have rushed to beat her, but Lieutenant Silva is left psychologically defeated by Doña Adriana's initiatives.

RG: Here we see a subject that appears a lot in your work: the power that language has to change reality. Doña Adriana uses words like a weapon to defend herself and to neutralize Silva.

MVLL: Somewhere, I read that in martial arts, a good fighter uses his adversary's power to give it back to him. An experienced professional uses the blow's power, increased by his audacity, to respond to his opponent's attack. That is what Doña Adriana does in this scene. This goon comes to her house thinking he is going to intimidate her, but she responds with greater aggression. It is as if, through language, she managed to use the power the lieutenant brought to turn the attack back on him. She expresses herself as vulgarly as a macho goon would, and the resulting litany is even more vulgar and aggressive than what the lieutenant himself could have expressed. Her audacity is such that he doesn't know how to respond and is left frozen. Doña Adriana's intelligence lies in that. What is entertaining is that in the end she laughs, she congratulates herself, and she finishes her tale coquettishly, telling Lituma, "Give my regards to the lieutenant." It is a moment of mischievousness that also serves for Doña Adriana's character to grow.

Alicia

MIGUEL CABALLERO-VÁZQUEZ: The novel's other women don't have the same power as Doña Adriana. Alicia, for example, lacks that capability to use language to survive in those chauvinistic surroundings. In fact, she ends up overshadowed by all the men around her. Alicia belongs to a higher social class but has more difficulties dealing with machismo.

MVLL: Alicia is a more mysterious character. It's difficult to know to what extent she is lucid, to what extent she is sincere, to what extent she is twisted, to what extent she is conscious of the things she does. What we do know is that she is more educated and that she is of a higher social class than the other characters, but that doesn't make her stronger: there are moments in which she seems very vulnerable, although, according to her father's testimony, she is a very large destructive force. Who is telling the truth? I don't know: it depends on the interpretation of each reader.

THE PROBLEM OF TRUTH

RG: *Palomino Molero* shows that an objective truth does not always come across as credible to the public. The reader knows that Mindreau committed suicide—this is one of the few provable truths in the novel—but the villagers, the townspeople, don't believe it, in part because they maintain that the powerful don't commit suicide: if they die, it's because someone killed them. Can you talk to us about that incredulous public, which is guided less by reason than by certain fantasies? That episode seems to foreshadow what happened during your presidential campaign: there, you also found people who didn't want to believe in certain provable truths.

MVLL: It is fascinating to me, the process of mythification that occurs in the realm of what has been called public opinion. Public opinion carries out strange operations that produce curious results: truths become lies, and lies become truths. There are things people don't want to believe, and at the same time they believe things that are not true. One of the great instruments in that transformation is literature. The literary versions of history many times superimpose themselves over history and replace it, as occurs in *War and Peace*. It is a novel so absolutely extraordinary that readers come to believe that things really happened that way, although historians have strived to show that Tolstoy took many liberties and that reality was more complex or simpler than the novelist's version. No one who reads Tolstoy can imagine that the battles he narrates happened any other way. Literature replaces the truth, as also occurs with the Battle of Waterloo narrated by Victor Hugo. This battle is narrated so marvelously in *Les Misérables* that in the end readers emerge convinced that it was the historical truth. Experts have shown that it was not like that, but the novel's persuasive force is so huge that it transforms lies into truth. This is what literature does: it transforms reality.

Something darker and more complicated occurs when public opinion imposes itself on the truth, transforming the truth into lies or vice versa. It is very frequent all over, although more so in countries that have a tradition of dictatorship, of demagoguery, of twisting reality. There, the borders between truth and lies tend to fade away, as frequently occurs in Latin America. On our continent, political truths and lies are confused to the extent that it becomes nearly impossible to make a distinction between them. This is what we see in *Palomino Molero* when people refuse to believe that Colonel Mindreau committed suicide. The people are surrounded by unsolved crimes, by situations in which violence imposes itself on legality, and that is why they are so incredulous vis-à-vis the truth. The irony is that when the truth is revealed, they take it as one more lie.

RG: Something similar occurred with the report of the commission in which you participated to clarify the Uchuraccay massacre.

MVLL: Yes, that story has a lot to do with this subject. Let's briefly recall the facts. In the early 1980s, the Shining Path guerrillas had spread violence throughout Peru. It started in Ayacucho, an Andean city in the middle of the country, which turned into the center of that terrorist movement inspired by the Chinese Cultural Revolution and the ideas of Mao Tse-tung. One day, the news reached Lima of a massacre in a very remote place, in the Iquichana communities, very primitive people located in the heights of Ayacucho, in the highest parts of the mountain range. A group of journalists—almost all left wing—went out to Ayacucho to verify if the massacres were true, and when they arrived in Uchuraccay, they were killed in a horrible way.

A huge scandal broke out, and it was thought that soldiers were the ones responsible. The left-wing press associated this crime with the killing of peasants perpetrated by soldiers. You have to remember that the army had been called to fight against the Shining Path groups that committed terrorist attacks throughout the country, and there had been several very publicized cases of soldiers who killed peasants protecting the members of the Shining Path. So the press attributed responsibility to the army for the murder of the journalists in Uchuraccay, and public opinion asked for justice and for those responsible to be punished.

Then President Belaúnde Terry, who was a civilian and had become president through free elections, named three people to form an investigative commission: the head of the journalism school, a very well-respected lawyer, and me. The three of us traveled to Ayacucho and spent several weeks interrogating soldiers, union leaders, and political leaders before going on to Uchuraccay. It was an experience that made quite an impression because we had a town hall with the peasants in that place, and, during a very tumultuous session, they told us, "Yes, we killed them, because we thought they were terrorists. We thought they were from the Shining Path."

So what happened, to sum up the story? The members of the Shining Path, to escape police and army control, would hide in the highest regions of the mountain range, which is where the Iquichana communities are. These are very primitive communities that at the beginning of the nineteenth century allied themselves with the Spanish and fought against the pro-independence forces. They defended the colony out of hate for those who led the independence movements. They had a tradition of violence. The Shining Path members passing through there would stay in those communities—which are very, very poor, in contrast to the inhabitants of the Mantaro Valley, who are relatively prosperous—and they would eat the food and kill the animals belonging to those peasants, would take the children to train them and demand that they pay protection fees to the guerrillas. All of this had created conflicts between the Iquichana communities and the Shining Path.

There were several incidents in which peasants were killed by Shining Path members, so the inhabitants of Iquicha had a town hall, bringing together communities from the entire region, and agreed to stand up to the Shining Path, not out of ideology, but because the guerrillas had become a very heavy burden for those people who were so poor. In addition, they wanted to avoid any problems with the police or with the army. So they stood up to the Shining Path members, ambushing more than forty guerrillas and killing them. And since they had killed so many, they lived in a great state of turmoil, awaiting the Shining Path's response, fearing that their members would come to take reprisals. None of this is known in Lima, or outside the high mountains of the Ayacucho Sierra.

It was precisely at this moment that the eight journalists and their guide showed up. They were completely uninformed of what was happening and only wanted to investigate the murders of peasants attributed to the army. They arrived asking questions, and the community reacted with a terrible furor: they surrounded them, they attacked them, they beat them with sticks. Several of the journalists spoke Quechua and tried to explain themselves, but it didn't help and in the end they were killed.

And this was what we concluded from the investigation: that the journalists were killed because they were worked up and were taken for Shining Path members. In addition, the peasants had a lot of *chicha* and many of them were drunk. It was not a deliberate crime to do away with journalists: it was something unexpected, in part because no one ever went up there who was not a soldier or a Shining Path member. And since the journalists were civilians, the villagers mistook them for guerrillas.

That was a truth that no one believed. We members of the commission were attacked with a ferocity that is difficult to imagine: we were accused of having lied, of having made up a lie to justify the army, of being on the soldiers' side, of conspiring with the government to deceive public opinion. Many years later, after the end of the Fujimori dictatorship, the truth commission was established, presided over by a very prestigious professor of philosophy from the Universidad Católica and made up of a team of sociologists, doctors, and psychiatrists. That commission's report—which is fascinating, by the way—comes to exactly the same conclusions we had come to twenty years prior. But despite the investigation and the commission's work, it was still hard to convince Peruvians, or an important sector of Peruvian public opinion, that things happened that way, because the idea that there are peasants who kill journalists doesn't fit into an ideological framework. There is a prejudice established that those responsible for any killing associated with peasants must necessarily be soldiers.

It is true that soldiers committed many crimes, but not that of Uchuraccay. It's very difficult to accept a truth without any mitigating circumstances. Nonetheless, that is the truth. But the truth vanishes when it must face public opinion that is marked by ideology. What happens when a person has a certain ideological framework and is faced with a reality that doesn't fit into it? The logical thing would be to adjust the framework, but there are people who prefer to keep their framework and change reality. This is a case that has a lot to do with the story of Palomino Molero.

RG: Could we say that the three members of the investigative commission had the same role that Lieutenant Silva does in the novel?

MVLL: Yes, of course.

RG: Like Silva, we're dealing with three people who want to clarify the facts, without any other motivation in the way. They don't receive economic benefits, or political ones of any kind. But no one believes the result of the investigation.

MVLL: The final result does not serve to placate public opinion. On the contrary, it exacerbates it, and we see that the hate for the military is displaced toward the members of the commission. For years, the story of Uchuraccay and the accusation of having defended the military followed me like a recurring nightmare.

RG: There's a moment in *Palomino Molero* in which Lieutenant Silva says to Lituma, "Nothing's easy, Lituma. The truths that seem most truthful, if you look at them from all sides, if you look at them close up, turn out either to be half truths or lies."

MVLL: So it is, exactly.

RG: In *A Fish in the Water*, you tell of another example of this phenomenon: Fujimori's advisors launch false accusations that your team tries to refute with logical arguments and material proof. That evidence manages to convince intellectuals, but not public opinion, which prefers to believe in the false accusations.

MVLL: This is a problem that occurs everywhere, but that depends in large part on a society's level of culture. There are societies in which it is much harder to make lies pass for truth and cultures in which public opinion can be manipulated less. Lies can also be passed off there, but they have to be subtler, less crude than the ones that pass as truths in an underdeveloped society.

What deeply distorts the objective vision of reality is ideology: the prejudices and convictions of the political kind. There is a framework on one side and reality on the other. And when reality doesn't fit into that framework, the latter prevails.

THE OPTIMIST'S VIEW

RG: *Palomino Molero* marks an important moment in the evolution of your work. The novels prior to it presented a very negative, very dark view of Peru's political reality. *Conversation in The Cathedral* is the clearest example because there is a world without any hope that appears there. On the first page the main character, Santiago Zavala, tells us that Peru has fucked itself up, and at the end of the novel all of the characters, no matter their political or social position, end up morally destroyed. *Palomino Molero* also presents a society marked by corruption, violence, and impunity, but there is a glimmer of hope in characters like Silva and Lituma, who have integrity, are not corrupt, are not for sale. That optimism widens and culminates with novels like *The Discreet Hero* and *The Neighborhood*, which present a very positive image of modern Peru: a place where democratic institutions have been strengthened, the economy has improved, and opportunities for the middle class have increased. *Palomino Molero* is one of your first novels in which this ray of hope appears. It was published in 1986, a few months before you launched your presidential campaign: What was happening in those years that led you to think that Peru's reality was changing for the better?

MVLL: I was not conscious at all of that optimism, although critics later signaled that, from then on, a less pessimistic view appears, less dark, less gruesome than Peruvian reality. It is true, but I was not conscious of this change at the time I was writing the novel. I thought of it a different way: since the story is so brutal, with the torture and savage murder of that poor kid, I sought for a way to mitigate the horror while maintaining believability. I always aim for the stories I tell to be believed, that the reader enter, get hooked, and participate in the game. That would be my way of defining believability. I used humor deliberately: the relationship between Lieutenant Silva and Sergeant Lituma, for example, is very funny and generates delicious language that is cunning and mischievous with a foul word here or there, that in addition reflects that creole custom of speaking in double meanings, saying one thing to suggest a different thing. The two speak in vulgar language and make many references to sex. And those two characters experience a story full of humor that serves as a counterweight to the gruesomeness of the main plot, which is of the poor kid murdered and impaled in the middle of the desert. After the novel was published, several critics observed that there appeared a more hopeful attitude about Peruvian reality and the human condition.

A FISH IN THE WATER

A Fish in the Water (1993) is a chronicle of the 1990 presidential campaign. It is also an autobiography of the writer's childhood and youth, as well as an essay about good government that shows how literature and politics have been Mario Vargas Llosa's two great passions.

RUBÉN GALLO: When you began to write *A Fish in the Water* in 1990, following the presidential campaign, you had been writing novels for more than thirty years. At that moment, you made a choice that must have surprised your readers: instead of writing a novel about your political experience, you chose a hybrid literary form that included aspects of autobiography, of memoir, but also of essay and chronicle. How would you define that genre? We know that *A Fish in the Water* is not a novel, but then what is it?

MARIO VARGAS LLOSA: Perhaps we should begin by my telling how I wrote that book. The campaign lasted three years, and during that period I devoted the majority of my time to politics. It was a very profound experience, very important, but also very traumatic, because at the time, Peru was going through terrible terrorism-related violence. There was a civil war between the terrorists and the armed forces, who also practiced terrorism themselves. And I saw myself involved in something that had nothing to do with the politics I knew and that was an intellectual world populated by ideas, debates, projects, and that consisted of, for example, debating different strategies for emerging from poverty, for reaching modernity, for creating a modern society with opportunity for all. To campaign politically ended up being something completely different. I lived those three years with great intensity, but also with great confusion. When I finished, I wanted to better understand what I had lived, I wanted to see it from a wider perspective, and it was then that I decided to write *A Fish in the Water*.

From the beginning, I knew that it would not be a novel. I wanted to give a testimony that would be the most objective one possible of what had been my political experience, so I started by writing a chronicle of those three years of campaigning. When I had already covered some ground in the writing, I realized that that book was going to give a very partial and very inexact testimony because I am not a politician—I never thought of being a politician, or of professionally or exclusively devoting myself to politics, ever. I was pushed by circumstances, and although I devoted myself body and soul to what I was doing during those three years, I always knew there would be an end to that, that it would last for a limited time, and that I would return to my real vocation, which is literature.

It seemed to me that a chronicle of the campaign would give a very inexact, very false testimony of who I am, because I never, even in those three years, stopped being a writer. That was how the idea was born of creating a counterpoint between the political testimony of the campaign and the birth of my vocation, which happened when I was a very young boy, perhaps with the discovery of reading, which has always been a marvelous experience for me. I recall what it meant for me to learn how to read at the age of five and to begin to live through those stories, through those little novels for children, which were the first things I read and in which I discovered experiences that I would have never been able to live in real life. The intensity with which I lived those readings extraordinarily enriched my life's horizons.

So I thought of making a counterpoint between the campaign and those years of my childhood in which I discovered reading and literature. I wanted to tell how, little by little, I developed a literary vocation in a context that was not very intellectually stimulating. In the world of my childhood, there were writers, but none of them was only a writer: they were politicians, lawyers, or professors who devoted what free time they had left to writing. I knew only one writer-writer, who was a radio playwright, in other words a sort of caricature of a writer. I wanted to tell all of this to counter the political testimony, and that is how *A Fish in the Water* came to be.

I had never thought of writing an autobiography: it was something that didn't call to me. If it ever went through my head, I thought I would leave it for the end of my life, when everything was more or less wrapped up. And I would have never done it had I not lived such a traumatic and unexpected experience of spending three years doing politics without having really wanted to. That counterpoint that appears in *A Fish in the Water* is something that happens a lot in my novels: two stories, very different from each other, that little by little come closer together until they fuse and turn into just one.

RG: It's a literary strategy, in fact, a very typical one of nineteenth-century novels: the two plots alternate, and at a given moment they cross.

MVLL: They cross and they fuse. It's important to point out that in the end they fuse.

RG: It's something that we see beginning with *Conversation in The Cathedral*, perhaps, one of the first novels of yours in which a structure of multiple plots that cross one another appears.

MVLL: In *A Fish in the Water*, the part that was the most difficult and even unpleasant for me—because it made me relive such a negative experience—was the political testimony. That affected me a lot emotionally because it made me relive the enormous violence in which the entire electoral process transpired. In contrast, I felt relieved when I was telling the stories from my childhood and adolescence, which I wrote with so much more ease and naturalness than when I was chronicling the campaign.

PORRAS BARRENECHEA

RG: The historian Raúl Porras Barrenechea appears in your memoirs as an intelligent, kind man who taught you a lot about how to think about history and politics.

MVLL: Porras Barrenechea was the best professor I've had in my life and the best speaker I've ever heard. I've never again found someone who speaks with the eloquence and elegance he had. He was not physically imposing—he was very short, potbellied, always wore a jacket marked by dandruff on the shoulders—but when he spoke, he dazzled his audience. His students loved him. You had to get there well in advance because his class would fill up and there would be people hanging from the ceilings. Porras Barrenechea's classes were truly dazzling: he taught a course with a very boring-sounding title, Peruvian Historical Sources, that was about the sources and bibliographies to study the history of Peru. The wealth of his talent as a speaker turned the material into something so dazzling that I came to think perhaps I should study history instead of literature. Porras was an extraordinary describer of eras, of characters, of situations.

I was lucky that the year I was a student of his, Porras was commissioned to write a history of the conquest of Peru, which was his great specialty. That book was to relay the great division in Peruvian history between an Incan empire that was falling apart due to internal battles and the trauma of the arrival of the Europeans. The publishing house paid for two assistants for him, and since I had gotten a good grade in his class, he called me to work with him. For five years, I spent every afternoon, from Monday to Friday, working at his little house in Miraflores. That experience was more enriching than all of the coursework I did at the university. I learned so much from his way of understanding history, from his extraordinary rigor in research. In the end, he delivered a work that was rather small given all that he knew, perhaps because of the extreme and scrupulous rigor he had in verifying facts. He was a man with a great passion for reading: he read the classics a lot and from there had extraordinary eloquence when it came to public speaking. That experience awoke in me a keen interest in history that I've never lost. I've surely read much more literature, but I've always felt a passion for history, as you can clearly see in the things I've written. Many of my novels deal with historic events or at least historical facts. They are literary re-creations of given historical problems or characters. Porras Barrenechea had a great influence on me.

RG: The case of Porras Barrenechea proves that to be a great historian, it is also necessary to be a good narrator. The historian should know not only how to find sources and consult archives but also how to tell stories. Only good narration manages to make historic events come to life.

MVLL: This is the case with Michelet. Michelet was a great historian but also a great writer: he was an extraordinary prose writer, and his books are read like great literary works, which explains part of his success. Something similar happens with Porras: it is a great pleasure to read him because of the elegance of his books—an elegance comparable to the one he had when he spoke. I believe that all great historians are also great prose writers.

HISTORY AND LITERATURE

RG: There are many historians who are read as writers today, as part of literary history. I am thinking, for example, of William Prescott, author of *History of the Conquest of Mexico* and *History of the Conquest of Peru*.

MVLL: Prescott, who never went to Peru and wrote from Boston. It's a really extraordinary case, and in the end he wrote what continues to be the best history of the conquest of Peru. It can be read as a novel because of how marvelously written it is.

RG: That brings us to another subject that you've dealt with in several essays: the difficulty of delineating a clear limit between history and literature. They are two different vocations, two different genres, but there are moments in which they are close to each other and meld or become confused with each other.

MVLL: This is a very interesting subject and, for me, very current. A few months ago, I went back to a novel I had read fifty years ago: Tolstoy's *War and Peace*, one of the books that most made an impression on me as a young man. I reread it with some trepidation. But not only did it not disappoint me, it also left even more of an impression on me than the first reading. It is an absolutely dazzling book, one of the greatest novels ever written. After it was published, there were many debates over whether it was or wasn't faithful to historic events, which in this case were the Napoleonic Wars in Russia. To respond to his critics, Tolstoy wrote a fascinating essay about the relationship between literature and history, in which he says the following: "*War and Peace* is a novel, but it is absolutely faithful to history, in the same way that a history book can be." Why? Because it seems to him that historians falsify reality as much as a novelist.

To reinforce his argument, I'll cite the case of Thiers, a French historian who favors Napoleon and who also wrote about the Napoleonic Wars in Russia. Since historians need heroes because a history book does not exist without heroes, they are forced to invent them, excessively highlighting the gestures, the deeds of certain characters whom they endow with superhuman dimensions. In sum, historians fabricate heroes following the same procedures that writers use to create their characters.

Tolstoy recalls that he has been criticized for lacking fidelity in his description of battles, especially the Battle of Borodino, and he asks, "Who, really, is faithful? What fidelity can a historian have when he narrates a battle? I have here on my desk the testimonies of Russian and French historians about the Battle of Borodino and there are no two that agree." Why? Because history is written from a subjective position: the French historian will try to justify Napoleon's defeats in Russia, while a Russian historian will boast, with a lot of patriotism, about the victories of the czarist army. These testimonies are so subjective that they seem more like novelized versions of history than like actual histories. Tolstoy says, "I've tried to be objective, but I am Russian, I am a Russian patriot and don't feel any shame in saying that I am very, very proud that we defeated Napoleon and forced him to flee Russia."

Tolstoy considers that between history and literature there is no difference except the title. A history book is presented as pure truth, while a novel accepts the fact that it is dealing with a vision, a specific point of view. Tolstoy is right when he argues that a historian reorganizes reality in the same way that a novelist does.

One of books that has left the greatest impression on me is *To the Finland Station* by Edmund Wilson. This delicious essay reads like an impassioned novel, with the difference being that the characters are not human beings, but ideas. Wilson begins by telling an anecdote—he does so with the same mastery as a novelist—about Michelet. One day, this great French historian found a book with a citation by Vico that interested him so much, he learned Italian to read Vico in the original. Wilson concludes that thus was socialism born. The socialist idea, the idea that there could be a society with absolute equality, absolute fraternity, in which social injustices are eradicated, is born from that completely providential encounter between Michelet and Vico.

From that moment on, Wilson uses several protagonists to chart the development of political movements that propelled socialism and its different variations—anarchy, democratic socialism, communist socialism—and recounts the peripeteias that befell the representatives of those tendencies until the moment that Lenin, who was exiled in Switzerland, crossed Europe and got off at Finland Station, in Saint Petersburg, to begin the revolution. It is a book that refers solely to real characters and facts, but it is narrated and organized in a completely novel-like way, and you read it truly blinded. It is a book I have read as a great novel, but nonetheless it is a history book. The same thing happens with Michelet. Michelet's *History of the French Revolution* is a book that reads like fiction: although the characters are historic, the narration gives it the shape of a novel.

RG: Right here, at Princeton, there are courses offered in the History Department in which the bibliographies include novels. A novel can offer keys to understanding history and can make an appeal to feelings, something that is forbidden to the historian. I am thinking, for example, of Erich Maria Remarque's book *All Quiet on the Western Front*, which offers one of the most direct testimonies about World War I.

MVLL: As also occurs with Barbusse's *Under Fire*, another impressive novel about World War I.

RG: Or with the Mexican Revolution, which is a very chaotic period, a very difficult one to understand. Historians have published hundreds of volumes to try to explain that civil war, but in Princeton's history classes, professors put Mariano Azuela's *The Underdogs* on the reading lists, a novel that presents a very vivid testimony of life in those years of civil war. We have, then, histories that are read like novels, and novels that are read like histories.

MIGUEL CABALLERO-VÁZQUEZ: How much fiction is there in *A Fish in the Water*?

MVLL: Whatever fiction there is, is involuntary. I won't rule it out because in any event, the organization of *A Fish in the Water* makes it so the book is fiction: you would never live an experience in such a clear, coherent way. You live it in a confusing, murky way that is a jumble of all kinds of events. To isolate an experience in order to highlight it is already a fiction. But in contrast to a novel, in *A Fish in the Water*, there is a constant striving for truth. There is a great effort for the testimony to be not only believable but also truthful.

When I was writing the book, I looked for a lot of material from the time that helped me to remember and identify certain things. Afterward, I interviewed many of the protagonists, with whom I had a very good relationship, and made them read certain passages so they could confirm them or add nuance. I tried to approach the truth as closely as possible, although in literature it is impossible to arrive at absolute truth. But I did make an enormous effort for the book to be believable, and even after publishing it I've continued to make corrections—of dates or places, for example—so that everything would be as exact as possible.

POLITICS: THE IDEAL AND REALITY

RG: One of the great axes of *A Fish in the Water* is the difference between politics as an ideal or as a collection of ideas, and the reality of political life, especially in a Latin American country. The epigraph of *A Fish in the Water* says, "Primitive Christians also knew very explicitly that the world is ruled by demons and that anyone who becomes involved in politics, that is to say, anyone who agrees to use power and violence as means, has sealed a pact with the devil, so that it is no longer true that in his activity the good produces only good and the bad bad, but that the contrary frequently happens. Anyone who does not see this is a child, politically speaking."

MVLL: It is a quote in which I recognized myself. In reality, it is an idea that comes from Machiavelli and that is expressed in the book that caused such a great revolution in its time, *The Prince*. Until then, all intellectuals, despite their differences, agreed on one idea: that politics was fundamentally an ideal that was put into practice through action. And Machiavelli completely revolutionized the Christian world when he refuted this myth. He recalled that politics is a worldly activity, and as such, to be successful, it has to leave aside ideals, values, to be practiced as a technique. To be a politician, you have to be practical, with your feet on the ground, and be guided not necessarily by Christian principles but by efficiency. And to be efficient in politics, everything goes. Machiavelli proposes a pragmatism that can turn to cynicism, that can degenerate into a complete lack of scruples for someone who wants to be successful at any cost. Considering politics that way, separating it from great ideals and from great Christian values, was a big revolution and that is why *The Prince* was condemned by the Church and put in the *Index Librorum Prohibitorum*.

What Machiavelli describes is something that I experienced myself. When I began the campaign, I was still naïve enough to think ideas and ideals took precedence in politics. We launched, for example, a movement—the Freedom Movement—against the nationalization of the banking industry that caused great popular mobilization and managed to stop that bill. It was very stimulating to think, "Well, if a popular movement managed to defeat a law that an important part of society thinks is bad—because it is going to undermine democracy and place the control of the economy in the hands of the government—that proves that we do live in a democracy and that change is possible."

But later I realized that in a campaign, ideas have a very secondary role, and values are trampled on. For example, I had said, "Well, let's be frank, we're going to tell the truth, we're going to explain exactly what reforms we want to make, and we're going to explain the price of those reforms so that people don't feel deceived." I thought that previous governments had failed because they made promises they never fulfilled once they were in power. We, in contrast, would never make unfulfillable promises and would tell the truth. But of course, telling the truth in politics makes one immensely vulnerable, because if your adversary doesn't respect those rules of the game, you can be crushed by campaigns aimed at discrediting you. I lived that on a daily basis: we would make an effort to tell the truth, but then a distorted truth was rubbed in our faces. That really chipped away at the popularity we had at the beginning and that we started losing later.

Another influence was the terrible violence that Peru went through in those years: I was running for office while people were being killed every day, to such a degree that, in the end, no one knew who was doing the killing, whether it was terrorists or the military. These were years of absolute and terrifying violence, and that made whatever one could say less natural. On the other hand, I was very careful about language—something precious for a writer—and tried to find the best way of saying things. But in politics, that is impossible: you have to give six speeches a day and you end up repeating common phrases that are pure rhetoric devoid of content, a dead language that doesn't express ideas or experiences. That caused me a lot of anguish because I felt that I was betraying my own vocation. But there was no other way to do it. I recall that the advisors would tell me, "Don't use such complicated words. They don't understand. Look for basic words." And if you look for the basic in order to reach a greater number of people, you end up saying things that are purely rhetorical and very superficial.

RG: In *A Fish in the Water*, there is a minor character who is nevertheless fascinating: the American political consultant who acts as cultural translator. He translates the political reality and explains it using abstract concepts, but he can also do the opposite: start with an idea or concept to then implement it in reality.

MVLL: The consultant was a professional in politics, and what's interesting about those who practice that profession is that they have no position: they are neither left nor right, not liberals or populists; rather, they simply work for whoever hires them. They start with the assumption that politics—like architecture or engineering—is a technique and the candidate who best practices it will be the one to win the election. From one perspective, the job of political consultant is completely amoral.

RG: In all countries, there is a difference between politics as an ideal and politics as a daily practice, but it would seem that this abyss is even greater in Latin American countries, where poverty and problems of development make it so that our daily politics are dirtier than in Europe or the United States.

MVLL: There is a huge distance between law and reality. I remember that when I was immersed in political activity, I discovered which country had one of the greatest number of constitutions in the world, and that is something fascinating. It's Haiti, which, from a certain perspective, can be considered the most legalistic country on earth. But it is also one of the countries in which all of the constitutions in existence have been violated throughout its history.

RG: Although every society needs a series of laws, it would seem that in Latin America we have failed not due to a lack of laws, but due to an excess of them. What can we conclude from an experience like Haiti's? Because we have to continue creating laws.

MVLL: The way to improve politics is to get decent people—the most educated, the most prepared people—to run for office. Unfortunately, it doesn't always happen that way, because these days it ends up being very difficult for the very talented to run for office, and they almost always devote themselves to other activities. For an honorable person, politics is a very poorly paid activity: you earn very little, and there is always the risk of judgment that can come later. There are honorable people who are very capable and very prepared but who prefer not to enter politics for those reasons. But that is terrible for a country because if only the mediocre run for office, the results will also be mediocre. You should criticize the state of current politics, but do so with the intent to improve it, which is a real possibility.

Politics is not perfect anywhere, but there are countries where it is more decent, more honest, more honorable than in others. The ideal would be to induce talented young people to run for office and thus show that it can be a creative activity: it creates more human and more decent conditions for the population, especially in countries like ours that are so deeply backward. That is why criticism should come from the perspective that politics does not necessarily have to be corrupt, dirty, and that it can be something much better.

There is an extraordinary case that is worth mentioning. So much is said about corrupt politicians—with good reason— but there are also cases of politicians who have shown great integrity. This is the example of Nelson Mandela, an extraordinary story. Mandela was a South African lawyer who believed in terrorism and declared that the only way to liberate the Black people in South Africa—80 percent of the population—was through violence against white leaders. He exercised terrorism and ended up in jail, on an island, where he spent many years far from everything. He reflected while there, recognized he'd been mistaken, and concluded that to build a better country, he had to abandon terrorism and renounce the idea of expelling South Africa's white community, because both groups of people should coexist in the future. But what was most difficult was convincing his comrades, his own party, of the need to change their way of thinking. So from that little island, he spent nearly thirty years defending the exact opposite of what he had thought when he first got involved politically, and what is extraordinary is what he achieved: he persuaded his own party that they had to include whites and also convinced whites that they could stay and co-exist with the Black population. That case shows that politics can also be done with altruism, with social sensitivity. Mandela did not use politics to become rich or to cling to power; he used it to produce a radical change that improved a society as complex and as heated as South Africa's was. He was a great politician who, in addition, was born in the Third World. He gave us a great example of what politics should be.

RG: Did you meet him?

MVLL: No. But I was on Robben Island, the little island where he served his sentence. I saw the cell and it shocked me that a man bore that atrocious isolation for so long, so many years without seeing anyone.

RG: Did you exchange letters with him?

MVLL: No, no letters, but I read many of his writings.

IDEOLOGIES

ERIN LYNCH: We've spoken a lot about the role of ideas in political life. What can be said about the relationship between politics and ideologies? Between the figure of the intellectual and ideologies?

MVLL: Ideologies are secular religions, as Raymond Aron said. They demand an act of faith and do not appeal to reason. Popper has an interesting thesis: everything that cannot be refuted is ideology. He considers that Marxism and psychoanalysis are ideologies, because they cannot be refuted, since they are closed within themselves and require an act of faith. The theory, for example, that class struggle is what moves history in a certain direction is impossible to refute: you either believe or don't believe in Marxism, and that is why Popper presents it as an act of faith. All ideologies work that way, like secular religions. Democracy, on the contrary, is the opposite, because it begins with the supposition that reality is not perfect, only that it can be improved. And since democracy allows living in diversity, this also ends up reducing violence: people with different ideas, religions, and orientations come to an agreement not to kill one another and accept participating in a very civilized process that consists of depositing a vote to decide who will govern, on the condition that the winner allows the losers to exist as a counterweight, as inspectors of what he does. This is a very humane system. Popper opines that democracy is incompatible with ideology, because the latter, like religion, only admits absolute truths. Fascism, Nazism, and communism operate in the same way: there is an absolute truth, which gives the right to whoever imposes it, whether it be through violence, inquisition, or death camps. Democracy is an imperfect system, but it is the most humane one because it allows for plurality within a framework of tolerance.

THE TEMPORALITY OF POLITICAL LIFE

RG: There is a big difference between the temporality of intellectual life, as we live it in a place like Princeton or as a novelist lives it, and time in political life, where everything happens very quickly and nearly instantaneous results are sought. What we do at the university is a great luxury: we can spend three hours talking about ideas, about books, while the rest of the world lives at the pace of Facebook, and Twitter, where you can't keep the attention of readers or users for more than a few seconds. In reality, the world of politics—as we saw with the election of Donald Trump—is also governed by the temporality of the internet and those social networks: it is difficult to keep the public's attention for more than a few seconds.

MVLL: In politics, ideas are replaced by slogans and the content is devalued. This is the most terrible thing an intellectual can experience. But we cannot conclude that running for office is not recommended for intellectuals because that would be an absurd conclusion. If society is poorly made, then you have to get involved in politics in order to improve it as much as possible. You have to get involved in politics so that politics becomes better than it is. You also have to recall that in some parts of the world, politics is less corrupt, less repugnant, less superficial, less frivolous than in other places. You have to work to improve the experience of political life in our countries.

RG: In the book, you talk a lot about the space to concentrate that a writer needs. To write, you need to isolate yourself from the world and be able to spend hours thinking, putting lines on a piece of paper. Writing cannot be done in an instantaneous way: it is a slow process that implies correcting and polishing before handing it over for printing. In several passages, you relay with great pain how during the campaign, you lost that space to concentrate, because it is incompatible with the time for politics.

MVLL: It was a radical change to my life. A writer isolates himself, creates in solitude, confronting himself and his ghosts. Political life is completely the opposite: it implies living in a plot in which solitude completely disappears. It caused me a lot of anguish not to have time, not just to write, but not even to read, for that activity has always been so important and enriching for me. That caused me a lot of anguish, so I would get up very early to read. And since I couldn't read very extensive works because the continuity was broken, I read poems for the most part.

I read a lot of Góngora, who, paradoxically, was one of the writers who had the least to do with reality. A world appears in his poetry that is of extraordinary beauty, created through language, which is the opposite of that world of slogans, violence, and promiscuity that one lives in politics. That little half hour of reading or rereading Góngora was like a breather that helped me to bear the smothering I felt the rest of the day.

I ended up discovering that I was the opposite of what a politician should be: a politician should have great passion for politics, and I didn't have it because my great love has always been literature. That was one of the important reasons for my failure as a politician.

THE INTELLECTUAL AS POLITICIAN

DIEGO NEGRÓN-REICHARD: I would like to ask you about the role that an intellectual can have in the political arena. In *A Fish in the Water*, you talk about certain collaborators who, despite being intellectuals, betrayed you and ended up weakening democracy. What role does the intellectual play in the democratic process?

MVLL: The question, more broadly, would be: What role do ideas have in political life? The intellectual is a man of ideas, a man who acts guided by certain ideas. It's a complex question because history presents cases of educated societies that suddenly appear to act by instinct, moved by passions that crush thought. An example: Hitler and Mussolini, the two great European dictators of the twentieth century, arose not in primitive villages, but rather in very educated societies— Germany was probably Europe's most educated country when Hitler won the election. It's true that he won with only a little over 30 percent, but he won: there was at least a third of the population who accepted the monstrosities that Hitler proposed. Mussolini also won the election. These two dictators came to power not through a coup d'état, but as a result of democratic processes that later allowed them to annihilate democracy. There were sectors in those educated countries that did not act in a rational or responsible way, but rather were pushed by primitive instincts to which those extraordinary demagogues Hitler and Mussolini appealed.

So we should ask ourselves: If in a country as educated as Germany someone like Hitler can win an election, what can we expect from Third World countries, where there is a great lack of education and where passions, not ideas, prevail in daily life? In these countries, ideas move only a very small minority of the population.

The great liberal philosopher Karl Popper, who also experienced Nazism himself—he came from a Jewish family and although he was completely integrated into Austrian society, he had to flee Vienna when Nazism surged—wrote a great book of political philosophy about modern democratic culture: *The Open Society and Its Enemies*. His argument, in broad brushstrokes, is the following: It is true that there are occasions in which educated countries and rational countries act irrationally, but behind that irrationality there are always ideas, although they may be mistaken ideas. Considering Jewish people to be an inferior race is a stupid idea, a mistaken idea, but it is an idea, not a passion or a feeling. This is a monstrous idea, but it is this idea that manages to move society in the wrong direction. The problem is not the lack of ideas or the rejection of thought, but rather the fact that there are mistaken ideas and absolutely monstrous ideas. The inferiority of women, for example, which is inscribed in the culture of certain Muslim countries, is a monstrous idea, but it is an idea. Ideas do play an important role in political life, and that is why it is so important that good ideas, those that allow for coexistence in diversity, that generate justice and equality, that promote democratic principles, prevail over the bad ones, over the ones that cause tensions, foment divisions, and create friction in the heart of society. This thesis of Popper's continues to seem valid to me: ideas always play a role, be they good, bad, or monstrous.

ARÓN VILLARREAL: Can Popper's thesis help us understand why Donald Trump came to be president? What ideas led to his ascent?

MVLL: Mainly, the idea of xenophobia, the idea that the foreigner is bad and what is homegrown within the nation is good, and that extrapolating it establishes the difference between superior races and inferior races. We're dealing with an erroneous idea—history has proved it thousands of times—that has caused sinister social conflagrations. When he declares that all Mexicans in the United States are thieves and rapists, he is arguing that the Mexican community is condemned, for causes that remain to be known as genetic or divine, to be a very dangerous race for civilization. In addition, his theses against immigration have been disproven by serious studies about demographic changes. If there is a country in the world that has benefited from immigration, it's the United States, a nation that was made by immigrants and that carries immigration in the genes of its culture. Its greatness is due in large part to the policy of open borders it had in the nineteenth century, which allowed it to attract the whole world. All the sociologists and economists are tired of showing that if industrialized countries want to maintain their very high levels of living, they need immigration. It is absolutely indispensable for countries like the United States, like England, like France, to have immigrants who maintain the machinery that generates wealth and stability.

But Mr. Trump is not interested in any of that, because he appeals to instincts, to the irrational: mistrust, fear of people of other races. These ideas have caused such catastrophes in the world that it seems inconceivable that in our day there is someone disseminating them and achieving great popularity by appealing to resentment and rancor, which is what the great demagogues have always done: appeal not to intelligence but to the fears and deep prejudices we all have. The result of their election can be catastrophic for the whole world.

EL: We've talked a lot about the role of the intellectual as a commentator or analyst of political life. But in Latin America, there is a long tradition of writers and intellectuals—to which you belong—who carried out political campaigns and, in some cases, came to occupy very important government positions: they were ambassadors, ministers, or even presidents. What can we conclude from these experiences? Have intellectuals been better or worse leaders?

MVLL: Václav Havel is an interesting example, which happened in Europe, besides. Havel was a playwright, an artist, a creator, very involved in political life and in the opposition to the socialist regime, who also ended up in jail. He played a very important role in his country and enriched its civic life because he showed that politics can be a creative act, fed by ideas. Havel never renounced creating—he continued to publish until his death—and at the same time, he did a lot to expand the rights, freedoms, and democratic institutions of his country. A figure like him makes us see politics as a decent and generous practice.

He was a man of ideas, but that didn't keep him from being very practical when it came to his leadership: he knew how to approach people, make them believe in the government, and that made him very solid and granted international prestige to his country. Havel was not the only one: there are other cases of intellectuals who have been successful in politics. Think of Churchill, for example. Churchill was a man of ideas, a great writer—I don't know if that was enough to earn him a Nobel Prize in Literature, that was a bit of an exaggeration—author of history books, and at the same time he was an extraordinary leader who resisted Hitler's invasion and imbued the British resistance with spirit. He was a great politician and at the same time an intellectual who lived in a world of culture. I ask myself how he managed to read everything he read while he was a leader: it's admirable. There are many other cases that prove that an intellectual can also be an efficient politician.

THE CAMPAIGN

DIEGO VIVES: What do you think you were lacking in order to have made it to Peru's presidency? Practicality? The ability to communicate with people? The dose of cynicism that every politician has?

MVLL: I was mistaken about something. We wanted to carry out a series of liberal reforms, and since we needed a wide base of support, I thought the only way to do that was by allying myself with two parties: Acción Popular, which had been Belaúnde Terry's party, and the Democracia Cristiana. That alliance was a mistake, because those parties didn't have a popular base to sustain them. I discovered that little by little during the campaign: they had leaders but lacked popular support. They were parties that existed during the election and later dispersed. The only true party that existed in Peru was the APRA, which does have a great organization that has allowed it to resist repressions and dictatorships. So I ended up associated with two parties that were discredited and bereft of popular support.

That was why Alan García accused me of being associated with the old tradition that represented the bad habits of politics, and presented Fujimori as a new candidate with fresh ideas and the ability to mobilize the population. I had a very concrete idea of how to reform the country, but unfortunately my candidacy was wasted because of my alliance with those two parties, and in the end it was Fujimori and Alan García who implemented many of the liberal reforms that my campaign proposed. People were fed up with old politicians and wanted something new, and that longing for novelty was embodied by Fujimori.

RG: What would have happened to you and to Peru if you had become president?

MVLL: The only thing that is certain is that for five years I would not have written novels. I would have written many speeches, and surely my reading would have been very impoverished: instead of literature, I would have had to read briefings and many reports. To imagine a history that never was is an interesting, but totally gratuitous, exercise.

JORGE SILVA TAPIA: In *A Fish in the Water*, you tell how the APRA launched a campaign to discredit you, presenting you as a member of a white elite, removed from Peru's racial and social difficulties. Do you believe that politics in Peru can be thought of as a practice that transcends racial and social class problems?

MVLL: I believe that politics cannot be completely disassociated from racial problems, and less so during an election period, when the worst weapons are deployed. One way to discredit a candidate is to link him to the leading classes, to the rich, to the so-called exploiters. During my campaign, my adversaries used this weapon very, very well. I've described it as a dirty war, which is carried out by certain means, and by those means the defeat or the success of a campaign is played out. In a primitive country, the dirty war is practically on naked display, while in more civilized countries it is done in a more discreet and covered-up way. Someone who has spent his entire life in politics is used to the low blows, but I, who was a complete rookie, had never experienced something like that, and it was traumatic. I could spend hours and hours combating the incredible discrediting operations put together by Alan García—who is a genius in that—preparing communiqués and rebuttals, but in the end the damage was already done. I was accused, for example, of tax evasion. We had an office of lawyers exclusively dedicated to proving that those accusations were false. And it was a full-time job because an accusation appeared one day and the next day there was another, and on and on. Some were totally outrageous, but we had to respond to each one, and there was a process for doing so, so we had lawyers who did nothing but respond to slander. There was a newspaper that served as a court to publish these accusations against me, and it did so on a daily basis, throughout the three years that the campaign lasted. It was a maddening thing.

I recall, for example, one night that I left home and suddenly saw, on a television screen, a photo with my face and the voice of an announcer saying very seriously, "Housewives, if you have small children, move them away from the television set because you are about to hear scandalous, horrible things, from a degenerate, perverse mind." I stayed on to see what those perversions were, and to my surprise the announcer read a fragment of my novel *In Praise of the Stepmother*, and later several sociologists and psychiatrists opined and asked each other: "What kind of mind can the person writing these words have?" And another would add, "Of course, he is a degenerate, his is the typical born degenerate." And they would do that day after day, and I think that in the end they read my entire novel on television. How can you respond to that kind of attack? It was a perfect and devastating campaign, and it worked as they expected it would work. When I began the campaign, the public opinion polls had me in first place, but little by little the campaign to discredit me chipped away at my position. One day, out of nowhere, they announced, "Mario Vargas Llosa's first day in office will see the dismissal of five hundred thousand public employees." I never said anything of the sort, nor did I have any idea where they'd gotten those figures from, but people believed it and would ask me on the streets, "But why are you going to dismiss half a million people on your first day in office?"

We're dealing with a type of political practice in which scruples disappear entirely, and I wasn't prepared for that. I didn't have the elephant skin that you have to have to bear the type of campaign in which responding with the truth isn't worth anything because the game is to see who can kill his adversary first by relying on slander in any which way. I never imagined that an electoral campaign could reach such extremes. But that is reality, and politics is done that way, especially in countries where there is no democratic tradition or strong institutions and in which public opinion accepts those tactics. In fact, many of those dirty tricks work because they entertain the people.

POLITICS TODAY

MARLIS HINCKLEY: We could think that in recent years, politics has gotten dirtier. The kind of candidates that came forward during the 2016 election in the United States would have been unthinkable ten or twenty years ago. You claim that you have to be an optimist and remember that politics can always improve, but doesn't it seem like reality is showing us the opposite?

MVLL: Let's focus on Latin America. If we compare the Latin America of today to the one of twenty years ago, there is an irrefutable improvement in the political arena. When I was young, Latin America was dominated by dictators; today, we have democratic governments in almost all of the continent's countries. In the 1950s, when I began writing, the countries not governed by a dictator could be counted on one hand: Costa Rica, Chile, Uruguay, and that's it. The rest were dictatorships, some soft, some hard, some brutal, but dictatorships after all.

Today, we have democracies—very imperfect ones, it's true, and some corrupt ones—and the only dictatorships remaining are Cuba and Venezuela. We have known how to develop a certain level of institutions, a certain legality, and that is great progress. Another great advance is the social consensus in favor of democracy. When I was young, the majority believed in ruling with an iron fist or in revolution, and only a very small minority defended democracy. Today, the majority of Latin Americans support democracy and reject any kind of violence, be it right-wing or left-wing. And although social justice is still very much in question, there is a prosperity that did not exist before.

These changes have occurred not only in Latin America. Southeast Asia was very poor twenty, thirty years ago, and now that region enjoys extraordinary prosperity. Many of those countries had dictatorships that have become very rich democracies. That proves that progress is possible: it's not something that is hopelessly lost. That is why you must act with certain optimism, thinking above all that it is possible to change for the better.

Another example is the case of Spain, which I lived through. When I arrived in Madrid as a student, there was a dictatorship and the country was poor, isolated from the world and practically underdeveloped. In just a few decades, I've seen the extraordinary transformation of Spain into a modern, functional democracy integrated into Europe, open to the world. From an economic point of view, Spain has also had very notable development. It is an obvious case of progress in all senses, although it still has problems to be worked out.

TERRORISM

VICTORIA NAVARRO: *A Fish in the Water* describes the effects of terrorism in Peru but doesn't explain the how or the conditions under which this phenomenon emerged. It is a very timely subject: every day, there are young people trying to enter the United States or Europe in order to plant bombs or carry out other violent acts. What is the root of terrorism?

MVLL: That's a very good question, although a complex one. Georges Bataille, a French essayist whom I greatly admire, described the human being as a cage that encloses angels and demons. There are certain periods in which the angels prevail over the demons, but others in which the demons rule over the angels. Animals are not like that—they behave in more or less the same way all the time—but human beings have that ability to change, to be very different. There are periods in which the ideologies that exhort extreme violence exert enormous attraction and can culminate with the rejection of rationality. In Spain, for example, every day women show up who want to go be the wives of the insurgents of the Islamic State. It would seem that they've gone mad: Don't they know what being a woman in the Islamic State means? Don't they remember what the Taliban did with women when they came to power in Afghanistan? Women were kicked out of schools and universities, and they were forbidden from exercising any kind of profession; they became the slaves of their fathers and their husbands, and they went on to make harems. Is that what the young Spanish women who go to Syria want? The terrible thing is that the answer is yes: that is exactly what these young women want. So, what is the mechanism that leads those young women, raised in a modern and Western society, to long for something that seems irrational to us? There is no clear explanation: they feel great desperation at the living conditions in which they find themselves; they feel so absolutely frustrated with the lives they lead in the marginalized neighborhoods of European cities that they come to believe that absolute religious perfection can remove them from the conditions in which they live. They lack enough perspective to see the atrocity they're committing and how horrendous their lives will be when they become part of the Islamic State.

Even the most intelligent people in politics sometimes renounce intelligence to place themselves at the service of their instincts, of their basest passions, and that explains the success of dictators. Another apparently irrational phenomenon in politics is that many dictators are immensely popular, as was the case of Trujillo, which is one of the cases I know best. The night they murdered Trujillo, if the people had gotten the conspirators, they would have ripped them to shreds in the streets. And thousands, hundreds of thousands of families held vigil over the dictator's corpse and cried for many days.

No society comes to be completely immune to the risk of these excesses: there are some that have advanced so much and are much better prepared to defend themselves, but all live with that small risk. We have to be conscious that freedoms, legal rights, even in the most advanced countries, are always precarious and depend entirely on us not to fall apart in a moment of crisis.

THE AFTEREFFECTS

RG: Have you thought of writing a second part to *A Fish in the Water* that relays what has happened in your life since those years?

MVLL: Yes, I haven't ruled out writing a second part, because it seems that the book is missing something. It tells two experiences, one of childhood and the other of maturity, but so much has been left out. I don't rule it out, but until now I have not had sufficient conviction to get to work. Other things have always come up, other projects that get in the way. But I don't rule it out, because it remains somewhat incomplete.

7

THE FEAST OF THE GOAT

The Feast of the Goat *(2000) is, like* Conversation in The Cathedral, *a novel about the multiple ways that a dictatorship corrupts a society. In this case, the focus is on the Dominican Republic
under the Trujillo regime, and the crimes of that period are relayed
by a female character, Urania Cabral, who has started a new life
in New York.*

RUBÉN GALLO: *The Feast of the Goat* is an eccentric book
within your work, Mario: up until the year 2000, your novels
and essays had been exclusively devoted to Peru, with the
exception of *The War of the End of the World*, which is about an
episode in Brazilian history. The territory in which you had
moved was basically Peru and South America. How did you
decide to write a novel about the Dominican Republic, about
a very small country, an island that is marginal, even in the
context of Latin America?

MARIO VARGAS LLOSA: I decided to write that novel after a
trip to the Dominican Republic that I made in 1974 or 1975,
to gather material for a documentary. French RTV had hired
me to write a script and do the interviews that would appear

in a program financed, in part, by Gulf and Western, a company that cultivated sugarcane, which is the raw material for rum and also one of the main sources of income for the Dominican Republic. I spent almost a month on the island, interviewing a lot of people. And what really left a mark on me was what I heard about Trujillo, who had already died over a decade before. People had lost their fear and spoke with a lot of freedom about the dictatorship, which I had learned about at a distance when I was a student. In the 1950s, Latin America was full of dictators from one end to the other, but perhaps the oddest one, because of its histrionism—and one of the cruelest—was that of Trujillo.

Despite having suffered through Odría in my country and knowing the stories of other dictatorships, I marveled at what I heard. One of the stories that most left an impression on me, and that I heard several times and also read, was that when Trujillo was touring the country the peasants and the poor, who knew El Jefe really liked the ladies, would offer him their daughters. Could it be true? It seemed like one of those typical Latin American fantasies. What do you mean that the parents offered daughters? And one day, during that trip, I met a man who had been a military aide, a member of the special corps of the Dominican army charged with protecting Trujillo and exclusively made up of selected officers, all absolutely trustworthy and very close to the dictator himself.

That gentleman, who was called Kalil Haché, continued cultivating the memory of El Jefe and would gather old Trujillo loyalists at his home and gather objects related to Trujillo. I went to see him and asked him, "Is it true that the peasants offered their daughters to Trujillo?" And he responded, "Yes, they offered girls, and it was a problem for El Jefe, because he didn't want to snub the peasants." He told me that Trujillo didn't know what to do with all of those young girls: he married some to soldiers but kept many others. I again asked if it was the parents themselves who offered the daughters, and he responded that, yes, that's how it was. I was absolutely dumbstruck and in shock that that was possible.

I also met Mario de Tolentino, a doctor who was married to Marianne de Tolentino, an art critic who wrote for *Listín Diario*, Santo Domingo's main newspaper. While we were talking, he told me a story that left quite an impression on me. He said to me, "I was a kid, and one day I was sitting at the door to my house when I suddenly saw a very elegant car stop across the street, from which El Jefe got out, Generalissimo Trujillo in person." El Jefe was a mythical figure for the Dominicans, and the boy was left with his mouth hanging open when Trujillo got out of that car and entered the neighbor's house, where the minister of justice lived.

"At lunchtime," Dr. Tolentino told me, "I naïvely told my parents, 'This morning I saw El Jefe, I saw Trujillo stop and go into the minister's house.' I saw my father go white with terror, and he said to me, 'You didn't see anything. You're lying. Get that idea immediately out of your head! Never repeat it.' And I saw my father in a state of terror, and of course I have never been able to forget that scene."

Another story I heard several times was that Trujillo slept with the wives of his ministers, not only because he liked them but also to make the ministers undergo the famous loyalty test. His collaborators' unconditional support reached the extreme of accepting that he would sleep with their wives, and nearly all went through the test and accepted that Trujillo would rape their spouses.

He also said that Pedro Henríquez Ureña, the illustrious Dominican who as a young man had been Trujillo's minister of culture, returned to his house one day and heard his wife saying to him, "Look, this morning the *generalissimo* came by. He knocked at the door and asked for me, and I didn't receive him. I told him that I didn't invite in men when my husband was not at home." And that same afternoon, Pedro Henríquez Ureña got on a plane and never again stepped foot in his country.

I left the Dominican Republic completely dizzy, asking myself how it was possible that a dictator went to such extremes, because no other Latin American dictator managed to achieve complete control of a society. From that moment, the idea of writing about Trujillo was percolating, although I was very conscious of not being Dominican and I knew that the Dominicans had already written a lot about that figure. And as in other cases, that idea became an obsession, and that's the moment at which I begin to write. I made many more trips to the Dominican Republic; I interviewed many people, from Trujillo's supporters to his victims; and I had the luck of becoming the friend of a very distinguished Dominican intellectual who had fought against Trujillo and been tortured. He helped me so much and, in addition, introduced me to several people who gave me very valuable testimonies.

I carried out rather detailed research with the idea of writing not a true-to-life history, but rather a novel, in other words a plot that was based on history but that allowed imagination and fantasy to play a main role.

There are readers who think that the novel is full of exaggerations, that reality could not have been so brutal. But although it seems like a lie, the reality was much worse than what I relate in the novel. There are episodes I couldn't relate because they weren't believable: these are events that really happened but that would be unacceptable to a reader in a novel, because the reader protects herself and does not tolerate a reality that is excessively vile or monstrous: her defense mechanisms prevent her from believing and lead to the rejection of a story that is too offensive. So I had to eliminate many anecdotes because their crudeness was unacceptable.

Trujillo belongs to the class of dictators who not only brutalize and terrorize a society but also come to seduce it. They manage to deify themselves, and the bulk of the population pays them homage. If the Dominican people could have caught Trujillo's assassins the night of the ambush, they would have lynched them on the streets. That night, thousands and thousands of Dominicans went to pay their final tribute to one of the most brutal dictators Latin America has had. And when I was in Santo Domingo, I met several women, already very advanced in age, who recalled Trujillo, with a lot of nostalgia, as a gallant man who dressed well, danced very well, and was a wonderful flirt.

Trujillo's case was unique. In the novel, I tell the history of the Adonis, the minister of pleasure that Trujillo had. On a trip to New York, they brought the president an advertisement showing a young man with a perfect smile, announcing a toothpaste. And they told him that the guy was Dominican. Trujillo responded that he wanted to meet him, and so they introduced him to Manuel de Moya Alonzo, who is the model for Manuel Alfonso in my novel.

Trujillo was left very impressed by Moya Alonzo's elegance and hired him on the spot to work as his sartorial advisor, because he was very interested in fashion. He was ashamed of being mixed-race and wanted to compensate for it through his clothing. Moya Alonzo had an extraordinary career selecting the suits, shirts, ties, shoes, colognes, and special whitening creams that Trujillo would put on.

Moya Alonzo came to acquire extraordinary power through his influence and closeness with El Jefe. He began as a fashion advisor and ended up in charge of procuring girls for him. Trujillo liked women very much but didn't have the time to woo them because he led a very busy life, so in his last years Moya Alonzo rented hotel suites and filled them with girls that El Jefe rapidly dismissed after sleeping with them. That became an almost daily practice.

Moya Alonzo was named minister of public works, but his real job was that of minister of pleasure for Trujillo. They say that El Jefe cried when he found out that Moya Alonzo got a cancer that destroyed his face, and he never again wanted to see that good-looking man who had suddenly turned very ugly. That is one of the thousands of stories in circulation about this character.

When I compiled all of this material, what tipped me over into starting the novel and organizing it was the following idea: Trujillo had all kinds of victims, but perhaps the ones who suffered the greatest affront were women. He used women capriciously: he slept with them and discarded them. And not only El Jefe: his sons also raped with impunity. If they liked a girl, they would abduct her, knowing that nothing would happen to them because they were the owners—in the most rigorous sense of the word—of the nation. They say that Trujillo didn't steal because he didn't need to: he already owned half the country. No business in the Dominican Republic could prosper if it didn't allow important participation by the Trujillo family.

They say that people didn't lock their doors at home because there were no robberies. Robert Crassweller, Trujillo's best biographer, narrates how, after a bank robbery one day, the president gathered the heads of police at the palace and literally told them, "Look, in the Dominican Republic, only one person steals, and that person is me. No one else. So this bank robbery is a personal attack. I want you to immediately capture not just the attackers but all of their family members." And so it was: he had the attackers killed along with all of their relatives. What a remedy! From that day on, there were no more robberies in the Dominican Republic.

When I reached the conclusion that the worst victims of Trujillo's were women, the character of Urania Cabral came up. I wanted to make that female character the book's backbone and to build the story around her biography. She is a character inspired by the situation of many women who were accosted, violated under Trujillo, especially the case of the Mirabal sisters, which was a real story. These three sisters, very courageous, from a little village in the Dominican Republic's interior, were resisters. Minerva was an exceptionally intelligent, courageous, and beautiful woman. They say—we don't know if it is a myth or a real fact—that Trujillo, on one of his trips, when he went through the village of Ojo de Agua, where the Mirabal family lived, danced with a beautiful girl who turned out to be Minerva. He liked to dance very much and boasted of being a great merengue dancer. They say that he crossed a line and she smacked him. That legend highlights the personality and courage of that woman.

Minerva Mirabal was very persecuted by Trujillo. He did things as perverse as allowing her to study law and then, after all those years in school, he forbade her getting the degree to thus ensure that she would never be able to practice law. She was clandestinely active in the movement of Trujillo's adversaries. I was able to speak to one of them, who recalled that exceptional woman's great courage and told me, "We were in a cell together and she insisted, 'You have to undergo torture first, before the police get you, so that you learn to resist, so that you learn not to betray anyone.'" And as she predicted, she was jailed and tortured. In the end, Trujillo ordered that she be killed along with her two sisters. They had gone to visit their husbands, who were in a prison very far away from Ciudad Trujillo, and as they were making the journey, which was many hours long, the Trujillo police's henchmen captured them, clubbed them to death, and then, to make it look like an accident, put them in a jeep and pushed it off a cliff. Everyone immediately knew that it was a murder, and this caused such indignation that it pushed at least three of the conspirators to participate in the ambush against Trujillo.

Today in Santo Domingo, there is a great monument to Minerva Mirabal, who has become a symbol of the resistance against Trujillo. That is why the character of Urania Cabral—although she reflects an experience that was very widespread—is inspired by this woman in particular. The novel gathers a large amount of historical material, but also a lot of fantasy. The only limitation I imposed on myself when writing the novel was not to invent anything that would not have been possible in the context of the Dominican Republic of that time.

During the writing process, something very interesting happened. A character emerged who kept growing, acquiring more and more importance than I could have imagined: Joaquín Balaguer. Balaguer was a young lawyer who was a militant in the opposition until Trujillo, during his first electoral campaign, called for him to bring him into his party. From that moment, Balaguer collaborated with Trujillo and occupied all the important posts during the thirty-one years that the dictatorship lasted. He came to be the minister of practically everything, ambassador, and even president of the republic, because Trujillo selected puppet presidents. One day, someone asked El Jefe, "Why did you choose Balaguer as president?" And he responded, "Because he is the only one who has no ambition." But Trujillo was wrong: in reality, Balaguer had such great ambition that he was president of the republic once with Trujillo, and then six times more after the arrival of democracy, elected through more or less free elections.

Balaguer was an extraordinary character: he played a central role during Trujillo's days and later post-Trujillo. He managed to convince the Americans that he was the only man capable of peacefully taking the Dominican Republic from dictatorship to democracy. And in the end, he managed it: a very relative democracy, but that meant an extraordinary advance in comparison with what the past had been under Trujillo.

I wrote *The Feast of the Goat* with Trujillo mainly in mind, but also all dictatorships, which have a lot in common. There is a common denominator in totalitarian systems, so I also made use of the experience of the Odría regime that I had suffered in Peru and what I knew about other dictatorships in those years: Somoza's in Nicaragua, Pérez Jiménez's in Venezuela, Rojas Pinilla's in Colombia, and Perón's in Argentina. At that time, all Latin American countries—Costa Rica, Chile, and Uruguay were the only exceptions—suffered under dictatorships. I wanted my novel to summarize the experience of the caudillo and to show how these strongmen completely expropriate national sovereignty to assume it in their own names. And I wanted to deal with a more delicate subject, which is that of the shared responsibility of people who suffer under a dictatorship, because of the ease with which citizens get used to the regime, and in many cases strengthen and uphold it.

It's a reality that ends up being difficult to accept but that is very clear to see in the case of the Dominican Republic. At the beginning, there is resistance, but later, due to a need for survival that is perfectly understandable, ordinary people become accustomed to the regime and allow themselves to be manipulated until they come to identify with the strongman, who does whatever he wants with them. The extremes of humiliation that the Dominican Republic was able to achieve under Trujillo are unspeakable. An example: When Trujillo's son Ramfis turned ten years old, he was named a general. There are absolutely chilling images of that boy, dressed as an army general, receiving the tribute of the Dominican armed forces and of all the foreign ambassadors, dressed in tuxedos. Trujillo presided over the ceremony, and his relatives wore special hats, some with feathers, and incredible uniforms, all designed by Moya Alonzo. Thanks to this stylist, Trujillo felt like the supreme arbiter of elegance, as Petronius was in the Roman Empire.

The Feast of the Goat is a novel that wants to express all of these things. And in it, besides a lot of historical material, there is also a good dose of invention, of fantasy, of pure imagination.

THE WRITING PROCESS

RG: Your research process is almost the same as what a historian or academic would follow. It's about making extensive use of archives.

MVLL: Yes, I begin with the research, which I continue as I write the first version, which is always like magma: a kind of chaotic jungle in which there is no order. What is there are descriptions, episodes that repeat themselves, but from different points of view. It's raw material that allows me the certainty that it contains a shape that is as if buried in a great block of marble and is the story I want to tell. And that first version that I write without being careful about style helps me so much because it gives me a certainty that I never have when I begin a novel. In contrast, when I have that draft done, which always has many more pages than what the published version will be, I can work with a sudden sense of security. I know the novel is in there, and that it's a matter of finding it, by eliminating some episodes and rewriting others. When I conclude that first version, I already have an idea of what the structure should be, of who the main characters will be. And then I do a second and, generally, a third version, which is the time in which I have the most fun writing, the one I like the most. The first draft takes so much work, but the second and the third ones come with such pleasure and I work with more conviction. All of those drafts are in Princeton's archives: I believe there are at least three versions of *The Feast of the Goat*.

LITERARY TECHNIQUE: THE HIDDEN DETAIL

RG: The literary device that moves the plot in *The Feast of the Goat* is secrets: the reader knows something happened that was traumatic, terrible, and that ruined Urania's life, but he doesn't know what it was until he reaches the book's final pages. That secret piques the reader's curiosity and incites him to keep reading. We see something very similar in *Conversation in The Cathedral*: there, also, something happens between Ambrosio and Don Fermín that is kept secret throughout nearly the entire novel.

MVLL: In all the novels I've written, there is always the secret that I call the hidden detail. The detail is always there, but it is like an absence that deeply marks its surroundings, that is more present than what would happen if it came to light. The novel always includes hidden details because it is impossible to tell it all. The important thing is that the hidden details be very multilayered, that they have a lot of meaning, that they manage to impregnate the story that is being told to give it suspense. Uncertainty is generated regarding what really happened because something is lacking. And if that detail is present by its absence, then the reader herself participates in the story and fills in what is missing.

Hemingway used this technique a lot. In his stories, there are always hidden details. It's what keeps the reader's attention completely hooked on the plot.

MIGUEL CABALLERO-VÁZQUEZ: As I read *The Feast of the Goat*, I had a more or less clear idea of what Urania's problem was, but the intrigue for me was whether she would reveal it or not: in other words, if the rape would be the novel's hidden detail. I wanted to ask you about that decision to relay Urania's rape.

MVLL: It was always clear to me that I would reveal it. If I didn't reveal that central scene, Urania's personality would end up being incomprehensible. It is a fundamental detail to emblematically show, to summarize in one act what violence was like during the dictatorship. The story of a father who offers his daughter so that Trujillo can have his way with her is something monstrous. In addition, Agustín Cabral loves his daughter and has a very cordial and healthy relationship with her. But suddenly, that shocking episode occurs and shows the degree to which the corruption produced by the dictatorship can deform a man.

At the same time, there are certain scenes that a writer can't directly present to the reader without preparing him first, because the reader is protective and if he stumbles across something that offends him too much, he won't believe it. The novelist has to soften that resistance little by little.

When we get to the moment in which I relay the rape of Urania Cabral, so many things have happened by then that the reader is willing to accept it all, because he knows that there exists an absolutely abnormal situation, that all excesses are allowed in that world. So the rape of Urania Cabral, no matter how terrible it is, ends up being believable within that context.

LARA NORGAARD: There is another secret in the novel: Trujillo's assassination is being plotted by the young men in the car. There is a juxtaposition between the two plots, Urania's and the conspirators', and in both there is a secret that isn't told until the novel is very far along. Can you talk to us about the relationship between those two secrets and those two plots?

MVLL: One of the characteristics of the modern novel, the novel of our era, is that the organization of time has no reason to appear to be chronological. You can take apart time and turn it into a space. Just like one can move through space, in the modern novel, one moves through time: jumping to

episodes that will occur in the future or going back to episodes that occurred in the past. In these novels, the closeness
or the distance of the episodes is a function not of the chronology, but of affinity or rejection. There are similar situations
that are simultaneously narrated although they occurred at
very different times, and also situations that are dissimilar but
that are narrated as if they were related to create closeness
between opposites. It's the opposition that brings the episodes
close together.

In my case, at least, there is pure intuition. I know that if
I bring together two episodes, they will enrich each other.
And separating those episodes in time will create a curiosity,
an attention in the reader that will be much greater than if
they are narrated chronologically. It is also very important to
me to maintain a certain mystery, a certain ambiguity about
the chronological relationship of the episodes. I like for that
to be clarified little by little to maintain suspense in the reading of the story, which is indispensable for the believability of
what one is telling. If the reader does not believe, the story
dies. That is why you have to keep alive not only the reader's
curiosity but also his sense of credulity. In one of his essays
about the novel, E. M. Forster said, "It's very important for
the reader to ask himself on each page, now what? What
comes next?" If one manages that, the novel has been achieved
and will be successful. But if the reader gets bored or dis-
tracted, the novel fails.

In contrast to Urania's rape, the episode about Trujillo's
death follows real events very closely. There is only one member of the commando unit that assassinated Trujillo who
remains alive. I visited him on two occasions. Trujillo's supporters tried to kill him three or four times: they shot at him
with machine guns once in the middle of Santo Domingo,

but he kept driving his car and went to a hospital. When I visited him, he lived surrounded by bodyguards who protected him. He told me that, like almost half of the conspirators, he had been a supporter of Trujillo, and he said to me, "For me, what was decisive, what convinced me to enter the conspiracy, was the murder of the Mirabals." In addition, he said it to me in a very macho way: "They killed our sons, they killed our fathers, but that they would kill our women, that was too much." He said, "So I decided to kill Trujillo because he had gone past the limits of what we could tolerate." He was a very interesting character, a soldier who had also been a loyal supporter of Trujillo for many, many years, with important positions within the army, until he was overcome by the murder of the Mirabals.

Another of the characters in the conspiracy was very Catholic and even went to consult the apostolic nuncio to ask if it was true that Saint Thomas Aquinas said that killing a tyrant could be justified. His son says that the nuncio didn't say anything to him, but pointed, in silence, with one finger, to a paragraph from Saint Thomas's commentary on tyrannicide.

THE CHARACTERS

Trujillo

RG: There are many similarities between *Conversation in The Cathedral* and *The Feast of the Goat*. The main one would be the project of investigating the effects of a dictatorship, the great corruption it produces in a segment of the population who would normally be considered apolitical: servants, chauffeurs, teenagers, children. This is in both novels, but with a major difference: in *Conversation*, the dictator never appears.

MVLL: Odría never appears; in contrast, in *The Feast of the Goat*, the dictator is the axis of the story.

DIEGO NEGRÓN-REICHARD: I wanted to ask you about an important difference between Trujillo and Odría: Trujillo hypnotized his people and got them to love him. Odría, in contrast, does not seem to have had the same powers of seduction.

MVLL: There are important differences between the two: Odría only lasted eight years, but Trujillo was in power for thirty-one years. Odría was mediocre, while Trujillo had a certain grandeur, a malevolent grandeur. Odría was happy enough to steal just a little, because he didn't even steal that much. I remember an anecdote: a friend of mine asked a taxi driver, "But you're going to vote for Fujimori? Don't you know he's a crook?" And the taxi driver responded, "No, no. Fujimori only steals the right amount." It's a magnificent expression: stealing the right amount. That's how Odría was: he stole the right amount. Luckily for Peruvians, he lacked ambitions, he never considered himself a redeemer. He was a small, corrupt petty dictator, a somewhat violent one, but you can't even remotely compare that to the evil of Trujillo.

RG: Can you talk to us about the decision not to hide Trujillo as Odría had been hidden?

MVLL: In *Conversation in The Cathedral*, I always felt it like a void that the dictator never appeared: the effects could be seen, but the dictatorship itself was represented not by the dictator but by the minor functionary Cayo Shithead. The novel even gets to the door of Odría's office, but it never enters. I was left with the feeling that there was an absence there. So when I began *The Feast of the Goat*, I decided to do the complete opposite: the dictator would preside over the regime and would become a main character.

When I was very far along in the novel, Kalil Haché organized a dinner for the regime's former public servants at a house that contained a desk and other objects belonging to Trujillo. And it was absolutely fascinating because those gentlemen, already advanced in years, spoke of El Jefe in an almost religious way, with a great admiration that allowed one to imagine what the adulation of Trujillo must have been like when he was alive.

One of the worst repressors—he committed suicide just a few years ago—was an aviation colonel, a very close friend of Ramfis Trujillo. When I was doing research, I managed, through a friend of his, to make an appointment with him. He had already retired from the army: he had lived abroad for many years, had returned, and at the time was running a business. They said he was Opus Dei, and he was seen taking communion every Sunday and handing around the collection plate. And he agreed to see me. He was a very cold man, as cold as a fish. And then he spoke to me. Of course, he defended Trujillo. He did so in a way that was not stupid, saying, "This was a country in chaos until El Jefe came along. There was a struggle between factions here, the country was utterly barbaric, until El Jefe imposed order. We had the continent's most prosperous economy. We finally had working institutions." I said to him, "Forgive me, but I want to ask you something. A Dominican friend, José Israel Cuello, who brought me to your office door, told me a story. He told me he had been taken to the famous electric chair and that when he was being tortured, you entered and said to him, 'Aren't you ashamed? I know your father, a teacher. How is it possible that you are conspiring?' And that then you had a whip in your hand and you whipped him in the face, which left him with a scar he still has." And I asked him, "Is that story true?" And it was the only moment in the conversation that I saw he was confused, pale, and he responded, "Do you want me to tell you the truth? I don't remember that."

I thought, "If he doesn't remember that it's because he entered the torture room so many times that his memories of it are mixed up with each other. Because he couldn't have entered just one time. The only explanation, if it is true that he doesn't remember, is that he broke so many detainees' faces with his whip that he lost count." This man was—along with Ramfis—one of the murderers who tortured and killed Trujillo's assassins at a farm in the outskirts of the capital. I could tell anecdotes like this one a hundred more times; they were my working material for the novel. The richness of the stories is such that the difficult thing was having to eliminate them and leave them out of the plot.

KYLE BERLIN: Trujillo seemed to control everything, but he couldn't control his own body: not his skin color, or his masculinity, or his bladder.

MVLL: Trujillo had a great incontinence problem. He urinated on himself everywhere. They say that one of his ministers was always sitting next to him and was the one in charge of throwing a glass of water on him when he urinated on his own pants: everything was left as an accident, and the president scolded his minister for the accident. It was something that caused him a lot of anguish precisely because he was so macho: it was as if he'd been punished through his symbol of virility. And he suffered a lot with this problem.

In the novel, I tell the story of a young Dominican doctor, educated in the United States, very talented, who sees him and diagnoses him. He tells him, "You have cancer. We have to operate, we can operate on that now." But Trujillo is so mistrustful, he asks for the best specialist in the world to be brought to him, who is Dr. Puigvert, a great urologist who lives in Spain. A group of Dominicans travels to consult this doctor, but they don't tell him with whom they are dealing: they say there is a Dominican millionaire who needs to be seen. In his memoirs, Dr. Puigvert says that he examined Trujillo and told him, "No, you don't have cancer, you have inflammation, an irritation that can be cured," and Trujillo responds, "Ah, so what the other one wanted was to kill me," and he immediately has the poor other doctor killed. But it turns out that he does have cancer: the first doctor was right and Dr. Puigvert is mistaken. It is something terrible: a young, brilliant doctor is killed for having been right in his diagnosis. There we see the value of human life for Trujillo. He lived with constant paranoia, predicting conspiracies against him.

EMILIO MORENO: There is a scene in which Trujillo tells Johnny Abbes García that he envies him because he would have liked to have had a wife as strong and as capable as his, because he needed that support at the time to make certain decisions. It's interesting that a character as macho and dominant as Trujillo would admit that he would have benefited from a strong woman. That conversation adds a more complex facet to the dictator.

MVLL: Everything was bloodstained with Trujillo. The woman who later ended up being his wife was married to a soldier, and apparently Trujillo had the soldier killed so he could be with her. When he came to power, his wife became the Bountiful First Lady, but in the streets, the people called her "La Españolita" because she had European blood. By the end, she no longer had relations with Trujillo and led her own separate life. The only thing that is known about her is that she was very cheap and sent a lot of money abroad.

RG: One of the subjects you develop in *The Feast of the Goat* is how power makes one drunk and mad. In his authoritarian drunkenness, Trujillo loses contact with reality and comes to believe that he can act with impunity, not just in his country but also in the rest of the world, be it in New York or in Venezuela.

MVLL: So it is. We see that madness when he tries to assassinate Venezuelan president Rómulo Betancourt, who is his enemy. The conspiracy plants a car bomb, but the attack fails and Betancourt appears on television, with his hands burned, blaming Trujillo. That provokes a great international scandal and Trujillo is discredited in Latin America and the rest of the world. With that failed attack, he signs his death sentence.

MARLIS HINCKLEY: The relationship that the Trujillo character has with language is fascinating: there's a passage in which the dictator is obsessed with a speech in which President Balaguer compares Trujillo to God. El Jefe learns it by heart and recites one of the paragraphs over and over again.

It is an almost religious use of language, like someone who repeats a prayer in a church.

MVLL: This episode is based on historical facts. There was a speech of Balaguer's that left quite an impression on Trujillo that said, "Up to halfway through Dominican history, God made sure that this country would not disappear, despite the pirates, corsairs, hurricanes, typhoons. But the day came that God rested and asked for someone to relieve Him. At that moment, Trujillo appeared." Trujillo liked this story, which in addition confirmed his image as a redeemer.

There is another important anecdote about Trujillo's relationship with language. When I was doing research for the novel, the director of *Listín Diario* told me that during Trujillo's time—when he was working as a journalist—the social pages were the most dangerous part of the paper because they were the ones Trujillo read. The dictator didn't read editorials, nor was he interested in international news, but he did read, and very carefully so, the social pages. That section came to have great importance if you wanted to know what was happening in the country, but you had to know how to decipher it. A key, for example, were the special treatments. Trujillo's mother should always be called the *prestante dama*, for example. I am sure that there wasn't a single Dominican who knew what *prestante* was. But that sounded elegant to Trujillo, so his mother turned into the *prestante dama*, in other words, the "very distinguished lady." Trujillo's father came to be the "distinguished gentleman" and so on with the other members of the family. The daily's director told me that readers always knew when someone had fallen from grace because they stopped receiving special treatment: the "very distinguished gentleman" or the "refined and distinguished gentleman" suddenly became "Mr. Such and Such," and that was a very clear indication that something had happened to that man or that something was about to happen to that man. The director told me that sometimes news came from the palace that said, "Such-and-such will cease to be called the 'fine gentleman,' and starting today, he will be called merely 'Mr.'" This caused terror in the person who suddenly read the newspaper and saw his name written without any qualifiers. It was very clear proof that he could be imprisoned, disappear, or lose his entire fortune overnight. And all of this happened on the social pages.

The social pages, which in any publication are considered the least important, the ones that only interest frivolous people, were the most important ones during Trujillo's time. You can already see the extraordinary deformity caused by a dictatorship that has complete control over the life of a country.

RG: Did you have access to recordings of Trujillo so that you could listen to how he spoke?

MVLL: Yes. He had a very shrill little voice. That is why he preferred for others to read his speeches. He considered himself the embodiment of the Dominican macho, but his way of speaking was not virile at all. It leaves quite an impression to hear the recordings with that small little voice that squawked.

MH: What relationship is there between Trujillo's personality and the machismo culture of the Dominican Republic?

MVLL: Through antonomasia, Trujillo prided himself on being "the macho," and his personality exacerbated machismo in the Dominican Republic. He was the total opposite of a dictator like Franco, who didn't aspire to be "the macho" or anything close. And Franco did not exacerbate Spanish machismo.

ALEXANDRA APARICIO: Could you talk to us about how you build the psychological profile of a dictator like Trujillo? Are we dealing with a sick being whose actions are a symptom of his delirium?

MVLL: To present dictators as a phenomenon seems to me to be a great mistake. It is an unconscious defense mechanism to say, "This man is not like us." But the terrible thing about dictators is that they are like us. They come from the place where we are all from, and they behave like normal beings until they attain power. It's power that brings out the monster, but we're dealing with a monster that we all carry within us. Dictators are everyday people who have been turned into monsters by power. It's preferable to live in a system that doesn't allow all of the power in a society to be concentrated in one person, because at that moment is when the monster comes out that lives within all of us.

RG: Trujillo is an example of the kind of eccentric dictator who lends himself to literature due to his excesses and his eccentric personality. Fidel Castro also belongs to that group. But there is a second group of dictators in a gray area, without any literary interest, where Odría and also Pinochet fall.

MVLL: Pinochet was a typical Latin American dictator. He belongs to the tradition of Odría, Pérez Jiménez, Rojas Pinilla. He was a military dictator who lacked charisma, an almost funereal figure, with those dark glasses and those rigid uniforms. Pinochet's was an institutional dictatorship in which the army assumed all power, including the power to decide. Trujillo, in contrast, was a big clown. That is why his dictatorship was so colorful. Trujillo's cruelty was also more unpredictable than Pinochet's: he could be pleasantly speaking to someone and order him killed five minutes later.

MCV: What was the ideology of Trujillo's dictatorship? In his final years, Trujillo feared, on the one hand, communism, and on the other, the United States, as well as the Church. Ideologically, he seemed very confused.

MVLL: A dictatorship like Trujillo's is not ideology: it is the dictatorship of a caudillo. For him, a good relationship with the United States was very important, and since the Americans said there had to be elections, he then organized elections and engineered them to win. One of the most grotesque episodes occurred when the United States really insisted on the need to hold free elections. Trujillo agreed and presented himself as the opposition candidate against President Balaguer. It was his strongman who won those elections.

He reached those circus extremes because he could do whatever he wanted with his country. He was like a sculptor who molds the clay to his will: he could shape Dominican society to the extreme of inventing the grotesque farce of running as the opposition candidate. His power was truly absolute.

MH: If the idea was to show how power corrupts, why doesn't the novel narrate Trujillo's life before he became president?

MVLL: Before coming to power, Trujillo was a completely un-inspiring figure. He worked as a goon at a farm, imposing order on unruly peasants. He had some aptitude when he joined a small group that the U.S. Marines trained to make up the Dominican National Guard during the U.S. occupation of 1916: he was very disciplined and very orderly. He performed so well that, shortly afterward, the Americans who had trained him chose him as the head of the National Guard. That military force was the only authority remaining in the country after the exit of the Americans, and Trujillo began to have more and more power. When they held elections, he presented his candidacy and won—we don't know if he won honestly or not—in part because he surrounded himself with good people like Balaguer.

Once in the presidency, he began to accumulate power and devoted himself to eliminating his adversaries and his enemies. The monster started manifesting itself more and more energetically. It was the accumulation of power that started making him an increasingly despotic and more extravagant character. I believe that is the case with all dictators. It is the excess of power that turns them into absolutely bloodthirsty characters.

AA: I wanted to ask you about the story of the accommodation between Trujillo and the Vatican that appears in the novel and, more generally, about the relationship between the dictatorship and the Church.

MVLL: In the early years of the regime, the Church supports Trujillo until it becomes a bulwark against the dictatorship. Little by little, it begins to distance itself, it becomes critical, until it becomes, in its final years, one of the opposition forces against the regime. The dictator takes on two bishops, one an American and the other a Spaniard, who had become his greatest critics. That part of the novel is very historical: there, I have respected the facts, although the facts themselves are novelesque.

Urania Cabral

EM: I was interested in the relationship Urania has with the Dominican Republic. As a girl, she suffers firsthand the horrors of the dictatorship. She manages to escape and starts a new life in the United States, where she studies, earns a degree, and obtains a very good job in New York. She has left behind the horror of her life in Ciudad Trujillo. But one day, she decides to return, and we don't really know why: she doesn't need to go back to that place where all her misfortunes befell her.

MVLL: Urania has a very strong psychological link to the Dominican Republic. There is an early trauma that she never overcomes, and that occurs on the island. The return to the city of her childhood is a pilgrimage to the origin. Her whole life has been brutally marked by that childhood experience, and when she returns, she realizes that she has never overcome it, that she has continued to drag it behind her, that her life is completely conditioned by it. Despite appearances, she is not free: she takes the Dominican Republic to New York.

When I went to Santo Domingo to present the novel, a letter published in *Listín Diario* made quite an impression on me. In it, a gentleman wrote, "After having read this novel, I feel the need to tell my sister's story, which is very similar to that of Urania Cabral. My family was very supportive of Trujillo, and Trujillo raped my sister. We were a very Catholic family, and that violation destroyed us. My parents left the Dominican Republic, but my mother never recovered and had mental problems until her death. My sister, for better or for worse, started her life over. Your novel made such an impression on me because it tells my sister's story, the story of how Trujillo destroyed my family, which completely identified with the regime."

I have kept that letter, which made such an impression on me. Urania's story isn't unique; it is something that, sadly, happened many, many times.

RG: Did you have it clear from the beginning that Urania was going to leave the country? Because that is an important difference from the biography of Minerva, who is one of the models for this character.

MVLL: I wanted her to leave because it would be impossible for Urania to have that lucidity without distance. She has an intellectual mind, she is reflective, she has ideas, she sees everything that happened from a critical viewpoint. So it was very important for her to make her life in another country and, besides, to have a successful career, because that would give her freedom and self-confidence in facing her father, who is the one responsible for her tragedy.

CHARLOTTE WILLIAMS: Urania appears to be the only character who has the capacity to make decisions about her own life, but even in her case, there are unknown forces that push her to return to the Dominican Republic. In a passage in the novel, it is commented that all Dominicans end up, one way or another, serving the regime. Estrella Sadhalá concludes that "the Goat had taken from people the sacred attribute given to them by God: free will."

MVLL: Dictatorships expropriate free will. The dictator monopolizes that freedom, and the bulk of the population stops judging, stops thinking, and cedes to the chief the responsibility for making all decisions, even the ones affecting their own lives. This is a characteristic operation of all dictatorships. In totalitarianism there is also an absolute concentration of power in just one person. Free will practically disappears; the individual ceases to be responsible for the basic decisions of his life.

When Trujillo would find out about an intelligent person who was against the dictatorship, he would send for them and say to them, "I want you to be my minister of economy, you who are such a good economist." And since you couldn't say no to Trujillo, all of his adversaries, all the members of the opposition, even the ones who most detested him, came to serve him and make up part of the regime. It was the supreme humiliation. Trujillo knew he had the absolute power to exalt his adversaries, to deeply corrupt them. It is one of the subtlest forms of vengeance against an adversary.

CW: And the effects of that humiliation, of that vengeance, continued after Trujillo's death, as we see in Urania's case.

MH: There are three female characters who play an important role in several novels: Urania, Flora Tristán, and Amalia in *Conversation in The Cathedral*. The three have something in common: they are the victims of sexual attacks.

MVLL: I hadn't thought of it, but it is true that the three are attacked. Machismo always manifests itself in sexual assaults. Sex is the terrain where machismo imposes itself and produces the greatest wounds. In the case of Flora Tristán, she was married off when she was very young to a man who abused her, who beat her. She had the courage to flee, which was a great risk, because at that time it was a crime to abandon one's husband, even if he mistreated her, and she could have spent years in jail. She spent nearly ten years in silence: we don't know anything about this period, not where she was or what she was doing. I believe she went to England as a servant. Her writings tell a lot about the lives of domestic workers; that is why I believe it is very probable that she worked as a servant in England.

Urania Cabral is very different: I wanted her to be an educated character, with a certain independence, capable of judging with a given critical distance what was happening in her country. That is why she studies at a great university and becomes a renowned lawyer, although none of her achievements cure her of her childhood trauma.

Sister Mary

MCV: Urania is part of a triangle of female characters, along with two other women who play very important roles. The first, who is a bit ghost-like, is her mother, and the second is Sister Mary, who is like a discreet heroine, who practically doesn't speak in the novel.

MVLL: Yes, Urania's mother is practically invisible. Sister Mary, in contrast, is a woman with more initiative.

RG: Do you have a real-life model for this character?

MVLL: No. Urania Cabral studies at a school that does have a real-life model: the school run by American nuns where the prominent Trujillo-supporting men sent their daughters, which still exists today and continues molding society girls. But the character of Sister Mary is invented and has no model in reality. I wanted Urania to go abroad and decided that the United States was a good place to see the Dominican Republic from another perspective. There are many, many Dominicans who have made their lives in New York and in other U.S. cities.

I needed a character who would serve as a bridge for Urania to reach the United States, and thus Sister Mary emerged. She is a minor character, but likable. In a world marked by violence and corruption, she is one of the most upright characters, the purest.

Agustín Cabral

MVLL: The character of Urania's father is inspired by a real character, a man who was Trujillo's right-hand man for twenty years. Trujillo treated him well until, during a trip to Spain, it occurred to him to invite Franco to visit the Dominican Republic. But Franco said to him, "I can't leave Spain because I don't have a man to be my right hand, like the one you have." They say that phrase was his undoing because Trujillo thought, "They see this man as my right hand, in other words, like someone who could replace me."

Trujillo returned from the trip with his prime minister, and the next day the Dominican papers began to attack the poor man, saying he was a thief, that he was inept. And then the prime minister, like Agustín Cabral, asked himself, "What is happening here? I am the second-most-powerful man in the country, and everything around me is sinking." He was accused of illicit enrichment and was imprisoned. Trujillo confiscated all of his goods. Two years later, he took him out of jail and offered him a diplomatic post in Switzerland, on the condition of never stepping foot in the Dominican Republic again. That gentleman went from being Trujillo's right hand to living like a poor devil, completely forgotten. And all because it went through Trujillo's head that he'd had too much power.

That gives you an idea of the precarity in which Dominicans lived, even the most powerful ones. Even power was precarious, because Trujillo could take it away without the slightest warning, as happened to that gentleman, over simple psychological resentment. Because there was no evidence that that gentleman was thinking of conspiring against Trujillo or anything of the sort.

The case of Agustín Cabral is very interesting: he is a very intelligent man, a natural opponent to the regime, but Trujillo forces him to receive commissions from the government. A dictatorship soils an entire country, and the only ones who remain clear are the heroes, who risk being tortured and killed. The ordinary men, in contrast, end up dirty because of everything happening around them.

RG: Could you talk to us about the decision to make Agustín Cabral a mute character? When Urania goes back to see him, he is very ill and cannot respond.

MVLL: The father appears as a human ruin who has even lost the ability to speak. If he had been able to speak, he would have defended himself and the novel would have to present the verbal duel between father and daughter. I preferred to have Urania launch a monologue, telling the story from her most private recesses. If the father had not been in that state, there would have been more tension and the story would have taken another path. I wanted Urania's story to appear in all its complexity, and that is why I ended up turning the father into a pair of ears. He listens, but we don't even know if he understands what his daughter is saying to him. I liked that situation very much, with the mute father, because it allowed me to fill in Urania's personality, her drama. I wanted to tell Urania's story, not that of Agustín Cabral, who is also a historical character whose story is already known.

The Conspirators

MCV: A difference between *Conversation in The Cathedral* and *The Feast of the Goat* is that in the former, there are no heroes: all end up morally ruined. The novel about Trujillo, in contrast, does have heroes: those idealistic young people who give their lives for freedom. In *Conversation*, there's no way out; in *The Feast of the Goat*, there is.

MVLL: The kids who kill Trujillo are indeed heroes. They know they are going to die, but they act from their convictions. This kind of heroism doesn't appear in *Conversation in The Cathedral*, where the leaders of the opposition are rather mediocre and, like all of the other characters in the novel, sink into a swamp of grayness and mediocrity.

THE COLLABORATION

LN: *The Feast of the Goat* shows a world from which it is not possible to emerge clean: all end up soiled by the dictatorship. Urania, for example, considers her father guilty, despite his having ended up being destroyed by Trujillo. Even if all of them are guilty, there are different degrees of culpability: there is passive and active collaboration, there are Machiavellian characters, and there are others who are completely cynical.

MVLL: It is true: there is a sector of Dominican society in which it is very difficult to establish the degree of responsibilities. There is a Bertolt Brecht play in which a character says, "Unhappy the land that needs heroes!" It is terrible for a country to need heroes, because these are always a negligible minority, an exception to the rule. You need to have a very special character to be willing to lose your life, to suffer torture, to give everything in the name of a principle.

The question of the responsibility of ordinary people is more complicated. Let's imagine, for example, a poor, very hardworking man who stands out in his own profession, and one day, the dictator calls him and assigns him a public position. This man can't reject it, because he would go to jail or be killed. What is his responsibility? He has a responsibility, without a doubt, but it's not the same one a torturer has. It becomes practically impossible to establish the degree of responsibility of each citizen with certainty. That is the terrible thing about a dictatorship: it soils everyone. The entire country ends up participating in the corruption and the crimes. It's the great tragedy of the countries that have had a long tradition of dictatorships.

There is a border there that is discernible. In the Dominican Republic, some collaborated out of fear, while others did so out of conviction: they were convinced that Trujillo had brought order to a country that had always been in chaos. It is true that, with Trujillo, the Dominican Republic experienced a period of economic prosperity: there was work and there was peace, although it was the peace of the tomb, the peace of the cemetery. There weren't thieves, people didn't lock their doors; you could go out walking everywhere, and no one mugged you. That security is one of the secondary effects of the dictatorship. Franco's supporters, for example, said the same: "With Franco, there was peace here, one could walk anywhere and no one mugged you, but now under democracy, you get held up, robbers get into your house." The justification for dictatorships is always done in the name of order, in the name of peace.

VICTORIA NAVARRO: If the dictatorship stains the entire population, it's ironic that Trujillo was so obsessed with cleanliness: he liked his uniforms well pressed, with white shirts. And there is also the example of ethnic cleansing: he committed a massacre to cleanse the Dominican Republic of Haitians. Was this a way of wanting to cleanse himself of moral and political grime?

MVLL: Trujillo was like an incubus. He had to always be clean, he who was stained from head to foot. To see a soldier with a uniform missing a button drove him mad, made him furious. He ordered terrible punishments against soldiers whose shoes didn't shine with enough luster.

HAITI

RG: Appearing in the background of the novel is the complicated relationship that the Dominican Republic has had with Haiti.

MVLL: Haitians occupied the Dominican Republic for twenty-two years, and in that time they introduced important reforms. They were the ones to abolish slavery. But they also left a series of traumas: Dominicans believe, for example, that during the occupation, Haitians raped all of their women. It is a nightmare that has to do with sex, as in all macho countries, but also with race. In any event, that episode has been left engraved on the Dominican unconscious, like a sort of complaint against the Haitians. People say that there are too many Haitians, that they keep reproducing, and that there are going to be so many that one day they will end up occupying the Dominican Republic. This fear of Haiti is very rooted in the Dominican subconscious, unfortunately, because it has been dragging itself along for more than half a century.

The massacre of Haitians that occurred in 1937—known as the Parsley Massacre—is one of the most grotesque episodes of the Dominican dictatorship. They say that Trujillo decided on it in a moment of drunkenness. He was with his ministers at a dinner where there had been a lot of alcohol and someone brought up the subject of the Haitians. At that moment, he gave the order: "Start to kill the Haitians. Any who are here illegally, kill them." What Trujillo didn't imagine is that the order, which he gave to the police, would provoke a kind of contagion and that the whole country would start killing Haitians. That is why the killing was ferocious, because the people on the farms threw themselves against the Haitians and killed almost forty thousand.

It was left to Balaguer to fix things, and he went to meet with the president of Haiti. What happened afterward was so grotesque that it seems like the invention of a bad novelist. Balaguer negotiated with the Haitian president, and the latter accepted that he be indemnified with a sum of a few dollars per death, for a total of half a million dollars, deposited in his name in a U.S. bank. In other words, the massacre of his citizens allowed President Sténio Vincent, another petty dictator, to pocket a small fortune. That operation, the fruit of Balaguer's Machiavellianism, resolved the problem. Haiti renounced making any kind of international protest over the killing, because the president was bought. It was one of Balaguer's great diplomatic victories.

Trujillo's hate of Haitians has another explanation. Trujillo's mother was a very simple Haitian, a discreet woman who didn't raise her voice, and he treated her, of course, with great reverence, with great affection, despite being ashamed of their Haitian blood. He wanted to be white and wore creams to hide his mixed-race features. He loved his mother, but he hated Haitians.

A few years ago, the Dominican Congress approved a monstrous law that declared that all Dominicans who had obtained citizenship through naturalization would lose their citizenship if they could not prove that their ancestors had entered the country legally. The result was that almost two hundred thousand Dominicans of Haitian origin, who had lived there for two or three generations, who had always felt Dominican, who didn't speak French or Creole, became pariahs overnight. There was very strong international mobilization, and even the United Nations intervened.

TRUJILLO AND THE UNITED STATES

LN: Another political background in *The Feast of the Goat* is the position of the United States vis-à-vis Latin America. In the Dominican Republic, for example, the United States supported the dictator even as it proclaimed the virtues of democracy in other contexts.

MVLL: Those were the Cold War years, and the United States considered that in Latin America, military dictatorships were a better defense against communism than democracies were. I believe that it was a completely mistaken policy, but that was the idea that prevailed postwar, and that was the reason the United States, being a democracy, supported Latin American dictatorships: it supported Somoza, it supported Trujillo. That began to change with Kennedy, who made an effort to support democratic governments and tried to distance himself from dictatorships.

Trujillo's problem with the United States didn't revolve around democracy. The problem was that he had Jesús de Galíndez killed, an oppositionist who he thought was Basque but who ended up being a U.S. citizen, and that created a monumental problem for him. This is a crucial story for the collapse of the dictatorship. We must recall that Galíndez was a Spanish exile, because this was another of Trujillo's farcical acts: as the governments of Mexico and Argentina did, he received hundreds of Spanish Republicans to show that he supported democracy. There were many Latin American dictatorships that refused to receive Spanish Republicans during the civil war. In Peru, for example, the dictator Benavides closed the door to them.

Trujillo, in contrast, received a ship full of Spanish

Republicans, and among them came Jesús de Galíndez, a re-nowned Basque, who later accepted a position in the govern-ment and was horrified by what he saw: he took note, recorded the details of the abuses he witnessed, and then used a pretext to make a trip to the United States, where he stayed on to study. He became a U.S. citizen—something Trujillo didn't know—and published a book about the Dominican dictator-ship that he presented at Columbia University. Trujillo be-came furious because the book talked about his sons—he tolerated a certain amount of criticism of his regime, but not of his family—and he ordered the kidnapping of Galíndez in the United States to later kill him. *The New York Times* car-ried out an investigation and discovered that Trujillo's agents kidnapped Galíndez on New York's Fifth Avenue and took him clandestinely out of the country, in direct violation of U.S. laws.

This was the beginning of the end, because the United States had Trujillo thrown out of the Organization of Amer-ican States. Before, he had had Washington's support because the regime was seen as a bulwark in the struggle against communism. Trujillo took advantage of that and labeled all of his opponents as communists: thus, he could jail them and sell the repression as part of the battle against the influence of the Soviet Union. The same thing happened with almost all of the Latin American dictatorships of the time.

Following that moment, the democratic governments of Latin America—Venezuela and Costa Rica—began to fero-ciously attack Trujillo. And from there, the dictatorship col-lapsed. Trujillo's response was also monstrous: he committed a series of crimes to erase the Galíndez story.

HOW THE NOVEL WAS RECEIVED

RG: How was *The Feast of the Goat* received in the Dominican Republic? I imagine that it caused very heated public debate.

MVLL: I wanted to launch the book there, and we prepared a special edition. When it was announced that I was going to present the novel, Trujillo's supporters published a paid notice in *Listín Diario* that said, "If Vargas Llosa comes, we're going to smack him." But I went and presented the book and didn't have any problems. Many, many people came to the presentation, and there wasn't a single cry of hostility. I presented it not just in Santo Domingo but also in Santiago de los Caballeros, and there weren't any incidents there, either. I signed books in public places, and no one ever insulted me or tried to offend me. There were statements against me in the papers, made by some Trujillo supporters saying it was a lie, it was all exaggeration.

An old Trujillo supporter, who had been one of my best sources, made some rage-filled statements saying it was all a lie, although many of the things that bothered him, he had told me himself. He wanted to absolve himself. But I didn't suffer any physical acts of aggression. By then, what was left of Trujillo's support base was insignificant, and I believe there was a fairly deep-seated consciousness that that had been horrendous, one of the most tragic experiences that a Latin American country had lived through.

RG: So did you have meetings with the political class, with leaders?

MVLL: Yes, of course I did.

RG: How did they react? Were they curious? Did it seem like a taboo subject to them?

MVLL: In the Dominican Republic, the conversion had already started. Many Trujillo supporters had ceased to be so and had become rabidly anti-Trujillo, in an attempt to erase and forget their pasts. But yes, I had many meetings. During the research process, I visited many Dominican politicians. Perhaps the most interesting interviews were with Balaguer, who, at the time, was still the president of the republic. In one of the conversations, I recall saying to him, "But, Dr. Balaguer, there is something I don't understand: you are an educated person. You are a well-read person. You have written poetry books, you have written history books. How is it possible that for thirty-one years, you were next to a bandit, a murderer, a know-nothing, surrounded by gunmen, by gangsters? How could you . . . ?" He, who was nearly blind, wasn't bothered. He told me, "Look, I had seven sisters I had to maintain, seven. I was a newly minted lawyer and poor. And I wanted to be a politician. What kind of politician could you be in the Dominican Republic if not with Trujillo? There was no other politics. The options were: with Trujillo or clandestinely, exposing yourself to be kicked out of the country, tortured, or murdered. And I couldn't allow myself that luxury." Then he said to me, "I made two rules for myself. First: I am not going to participate in any of Trujillo's orgies. And I've honored that. I was never invited to any of his parties." It seems that everyone recognizes that. He had remained single, he had been an extremely chaste man.

"That was the first one," he continued. "And the second rule that I set out for myself was that I wasn't going to steal. I've never stolen, and I don't have anything, except this house that El Jefe gave me, because no one could reject his gifts. But I don't have anything else. I don't have a penny saved, and I have always lived off of my salary." And it was true. Balaguer hadn't been interested in stealing, he wasn't interested in orgies, he wasn't interested in women. The only thing that interested him was power, and he was always in power. He even managed to fool Trujillo, making him think he lacked ambitions, and Trujillo made him president. In fact, he was president of the republic—although a puppet president—when Trujillo was killed.

And that astute man, so absolutely Machiavellian, who had been Trujillo's right hand, following El Jefe's death had managed to become the man who democratized the Dominican Republic, who brought freedom, who called for the first elections. He is a fascinating character who could be the protagonist of another novel. It was very interesting to converse with him because he told me many things about Trujillo.

He told me that Trujillo had given the order that no one take money out of the Dominican Republic at the time when problems with the United States began. That was very serious for the family, who wanted to have accounts abroad, because they felt that time was running out for them. Balaguer played a fundamental role there: behind Trujillo's back and in complicity with Trujillo's wife, he began to take money out. And then a marvelous story happened. Trujillo's wife was a scrooge. She mistrusted not only Trujillo but also her children, and wanted the money to only be in her name. So Balaguer helped her: he took money out for her and deposited it in Swiss banks, without her sons finding out. And on their end, Ramfis and Radhamés also took money out in secret to deposit in separate accounts. When the assassins killed Trujillo and his children went into exile, they desperately asked their mother to tell them where the secret accounts were. And apparently she, following the trauma of her husband's assassination, suffered advanced arteriosclerosis and forgot the numbers and the passcodes. For a long time, Ramfis, Radhamés, and Angelita, the three siblings, took their mother around the world, trying to make her remember the numbers of those accounts. And finally, the mother died without revealing the passwords and the fortune she had taken out remained in the bank. It's a marvelous story: Trujillo financing Swiss bankers, making them rich with the money he stole from the Dominicans.

The story of the children is also amazing. It is worth remembering the story of Radhamés, who was the family idiot. Ramfis was intelligent—he was fresh, a bandit, but intelligent. In contrast, the younger brother was an imbecile: when he escaped, he went to Spain and did some business with people who stole every last thing from him. He lost everything he had, and from there he went to Panama, where he lived very modestly. And one day, he disappeared. Then calls were made to find out what happened to the general's son. At that moment, a notice appeared in a Colombian newspaper that said: "Mr. Radhamés Trujillo Martínez, who worked in our organization, tried to swindle us. He has been clandestinely brought to Colombia, judged, found guilty, and executed." It turned out that Radhamés worked for the Colombian mafia and wanted to pull one over on the capos, but since he was an idiot, he was found out: they kidnapped him, took him to Colombia, and killed him. Well, that's the official story of Radhamés Trujillo, although in the Dominican Republic, they say it was all made up, that the dictator's son wasn't as much of an idiot as they thought, that he himself spread that story but that in reality what had happened was that he had plastic surgery to change his face, and that in the end he went to Switzerland to enjoy his money.

The older brother—who was more intelligent, but also a bandit of the worst kind—died in suspicious circumstances, in a car accident, at dawn, in front of Madrid's Barajas airport. At the time, Ramfis had invited several Dominican generals to visit him in Spain, and they say he was putting together a conspiracy. One of the legends about his death maintains that the accident was forged by Balaguer and financed by the CIA to avoid the return of Trujillo's supporters.

There is a last, very entertaining anecdote about the dictator's daughter Angelita. She had been married to Colonel Luis José León Estévez, who was another bandit. When her father went down, she went with her brothers to Europe and, years later, went on her own to Miami, where she converted to Protestantism and became a born-again Christian. She was seen on Saturdays and Sundays singing biblical hymns in Haitian neighborhoods at the edges of Miami. That is the story of Angelita Trujillo.

The story of his little children is almost as entertaining as the story of the little father. There are many legends, but the interesting thing is that the saga of the Trujillos goes on and on and on.

RG: Did you talk to the members of the Trujillo family at any point in your research?

MVLL: Yes. When we presented the book in Madrid, a very young woman came up to me and said, "It's a real pleasure to meet you. I am so-and-so Trujillo." I asked her, "Your last name is Trujillo?" And she responded, "I'm Trujillo's granddaughter. I'm the daughter of Ramfis Trujillo." I told her I was very surprised that a granddaughter would attend the presentation of a book that is so critical of her grandfather, but she responded, "I know those things are true, that my grandfather committed those atrocities." She told me she lived in Madrid and made a living as a flamenco dancing teacher. She was the daughter of Ramfis Trujillo and his first wife, Octavia.

THE LANGUAGE OF THE DICTATORSHIP

RG: *The Feast of the Goat* shows how language is used in a dictatorship. Toward the end of the novel, when Urania's rape is being forged, Manuel Alfonso tells Senator Cabral what is going to happen to his daughter, describing it as if it were a very great honor and using heroic, epic language, with nearly religious tones to describe brutality.

MVLL: It's a crude rape.

RG: It's a subject we already saw in *Conversation in The Cathedral*: the use of exalted language to cover up dirty acts.

MVLL: To read Dominican magazines or newspapers from the Trujillo time period is to enter unreality, to enter a world of terror that words dress up until it becomes its opposite, a happy, ordered country, peaceful, safe. This is the image the magazines offered, that the media in general of the Dominican Republic offered, and that some Trujillo supporters still have: that the regime was an ordered society in which there were no thieves or criminals.

DISGUST AND DICTATORSHIP

RG: There is another subject that is very present in almost all of your novels: disgust. In *Conversation in The Cathedral*, Amalia feels disgust when she discovers sex; Hortensia says that Don Fermín disgusts her. But in no book is the concept of disgust explored as much as in *The Feast of the Goat*. The novel not only describes disgust as a subject but also manages to produce that feeling in the reader—one that remains for a long time after reading. There are many episodes that produce disgust: Urania's rape, but also details such as the description of constitutionalist Beodo, who is fat with hairy ears and big jowls, who in addition uses completely repugnant language, full of curses. I wanted to ask you about that work with disgust. Was it something conscious or something that happened along the way?

MVLL: Dictatorships produce great revulsion in me, and dictators have always seemed like grotesque characters to me. In addition, they've done a lot of damage; they've sunk and ruined so many countries: they have been the tragedy of Latin America. And all have a grotesque physical aspect: lies, the reasons they use to explain themselves, the duplicity in which they force citizens to live, the unreality created in the press, in speeches, in official life. Everything becomes a great farce. That feeling of repugnance comes through in novels and is cemented in some characters and some situations.

The Chilean critic David Gallagher wrote an essay about *Conversation in The Cathedral* that I was quite impressed by. It tries to prove that the novel's central idea is that power is dirty: it produces a kind of pus that comes to infect all of society. And he shows via many examples that that rottenness even affects the prose of the novel. Language, when it comes in touch with power, is soiled: it becomes more vulgar, uses similes or symbols of the disgusting.

I never thought that, nor did I do so consciously, but the examples he gives seem very convincing to me. The characters, as they approach the powerful, start speaking in a way that is more tangled up and less coherent. There is like a confusion in the vocabulary, in phrases. And when they are distanced from power, the prose again becomes more eloquent, more transparent. This shows my state of mind when I was writing this story.

RG: Among the passages of *The Feast of the Goat* that produce a feeling of repugnance in the reader, the torture scenes stand out. This is an important difference between this novel and *Conversation in The Cathedral*, where we never directly see torture: the reader knows there is violence but never has direct access to the moment at which it occurs.

MVLL: In the Dominican Republic, I had access to very direct testimonies, told live, by people who suffered torture. In addition, violence was not used in such a systematic way during Odría's dictatorship: in Peru, the torture was cruder, more of something that was made up on the spot. In the case of the Dominican Republic, it was almost scientific, thanks to the character of Johnny Abbes.

Johnny Abbes is Cayo Bermúdez's counterpart, and both were inspired by real models. All dictatorships create the kind of character who, from the shadows, exercises a dark ability that consists of organizing repression, of using violence, fear, and torture to sustain the regime. Generally, they're uninspiring figures who are insignificant until the moment they come to power and become monsters. It's as if they carried a demon inside that only manifests itself at the moment at which they arrive at the peak of power, and from there they become indispensable to the dictator.

PAST AND FUTURE OF DICTATORSHIPS

MCV: *Conversation in The Cathedral* and *The Feast of the Goat* are two novels about dictatorships that deal with very different historical moments: the first was published in 1969 and portrays the Peru of the 1950s; the second was published in 2000 and describes a dictatorship that ended in 1961. What is the significance of narrating a dictatorship so many years after it has finished? Especially in the Dominican case, because in 2000, there was already a democratic government.

MVLL: The context of the Dominican Republic in the year 2000 is very different from that of Peru when *Conversation in The Cathedral* was published in 1969. But the subject of the dictatorship, unfortunately, will never cease to be current. How many dictatorships are there? In Latin America there are now many fewer than there once were, but in the world there are still a great many. No country, no matter how advanced it is, is completely immune to a dictatorship. The possibility always exists that, despite institutions, a demagogue or a fascist will come to power. Who would have imagined at the time of Rómulo Betancourt that Venezuela would fall into what today is the government of Nicolás Maduro? Venezuela seemed to be a country that was completely democratic, that respected institutions, that was inseparable from the rule of law. It had freed itself of the dictatorship of Pérez Jiménez; it had achieved democratic continuity. It's true that there was a lot of corruption, unfortunately, but no one would have imagined that Venezuela was going to become a dictatorship. It also seemed impossible in Chile. Chile was a very democratic country, with a legalist culture, and no one would have thought in the 1950s or '60s that a figure like Pinochet would come to power.

Dictatorships are not a phenomenon of the past. They are still there, very present, as a latent danger that can manifest itself at any moment. From among all the institutions of civilization, democracy is one of the most fragile: it is a very fine film that can be broken and leave exposed humanity's oldest tradition, that of dictatorship. Democracy is a modern phenomenon, very recent and very localized. The archaic tradition is the club, the brute force, authoritarianism.

RG: Mario, if you felt moved to write another novel about a dictator, whom would you choose? What other dictator would you like to explore through fiction?

MVLL: In the future, dictators probably won't be the brass hats with a gun at the hip that we saw in the twentieth century. The dictatorships of the future will be technological bureaucracies, very advanced, that little by little will expropriate individuals' sovereignty. In the hands of power, technology can exert dictatorship in a nearly invisible way, maintaining the appearance of legitimacy. It is a very real and very serious threat, against which we have no weapons to fight. Today's world produces more and more specialists and fewer humanists, more technocrats and fewer intellectuals. This situation opens the path for the types of dictatorships that George Orwell and others imagined. The dictatorship of the future will be practically invisible and will end up being very difficult to fight.

Technology can create that type of dictatorship if we don't humanize it: we're dealing with a technology that is more and more autonomous, more powerful, more widespread. To write about a dictatorship of our times, we would have to think about a dictatorship of that nature. The Trujillo-type dictatorships are more and more anachronistic, although some remain: Robert Mugabe, for example, the African Trujillo who has been in power for forty years.

8

THE THREAT OF TERRORISM IN THE
TWENTY-FIRST CENTURY

On November 19, 2015, six days after the attack in which a group of terrorists killed dozens of young people at the Bataclan concert hall in Paris, I organized a conference at Princeton to talk about the role of the intellectual in the face of the ever more real threat of terrorism. Mario Vargas Llosa participated, as well as the journalist Philippe Lançon, who was seriously wounded during the attack on the offices of the satirical weekly Charlie Hebdo.

Charlie Hebdo *had turned into one of the main objects of Islamic terrorism ever since the weekly decided to reprint the caricatures of the Prophet Muhammad that had caused great controversy in Denmark. Since then, the offices of* Charlie Hebdo *and several of its collaborators had police protection. On January 7, 2015, two terrorists burst into the offices and killed almost all the members of the editorial staff. Philippe Lançon spent several months at the hospital and, after undergoing thirteen operations, he traveled to Princeton in November 2015 for his first public appearance after the attack.*

PHILIPPE LANÇON: As the framework for our debate about terrorism, I'd like to talk about what a meeting was like of the editorial board of *Charlie Hebdo*. Until 2015, we were a paper that had a very low circulation—a leftist weekly of caricatures, with a run of thirty thousand copies—but that occupied an important place in the history of the satirical press in France.

On January 7, 2015, the editorial staff had its first meeting of the year, and there were more people than usual, although it was still a very small group of collaborators and friends, led by the caricaturist Charb. That day, we had a very intense debate about *Submission*, Michel Houellebecq's novel, which imagines a future in which an Islamist party comes to power in France. It seemed very good and entertaining to me, but many considered the book racist and in poor taste, in part because of the very complicated history France has had with its Arab minorities. That was the main subject of the day, and the debate was very heated.

Cabu, who was one of the most important caricature artists in the medium, spoke against the novel and criticized Houellebecq, whom he considered a reactionary and a fascist. All of us at the paper were very bothered by how little the state had done for the poorest inhabitants on the margins, many of them people of Arab or African origins who had not managed to integrate into French society.

Later, around eleven in the morning, another colleague, the caricature artist Tignous, spoke very eloquently about how these minorities were living in a very precarious economic and cultural situation, without society or the state taking any interest in them. Bernard Maris—a very well-known economist who published in *Charlie* under the pseudonym Oncle Bernard—responded to him, saying that that was not true, that throughout the last thirty years France had done everything possible to help minorities. Tignous did not agree:

he had been raised on the margins and had seen many of his friends fall into the most absolute misery. His response to Maris was very firm and very eloquent.

After that fight, as always happened, someone made a joke and everyone laughed. The meeting ended and I was about to leave, but I had a book with me about the jazz musicians who had played at the Blue Note, with photos by Francis Wolff, and I stayed for a few more minutes to show it to Cabu, who was a big jazz fan. That saved my life, because I spent two more minutes in the newsroom. If at that moment, I had left there, I would have run into the two killers in the hallway and they would have surely killed me on the spot.

So up until this point, it had been a day like any other at a newspaper that functioned like all newspapers in Paris. Suddenly, the door opened and into the newsroom came two guys with masks, dressed in black, with machine guns. They looked like a caricature of terrorists. I heard the gunshots, which sounded like firecrackers or fireworks, and then a woman's screams. There were twelve of us, trapped in a room that was not much larger than 250 square feet. We had no exit because the killers had entered through the two doors and started firing before we could realize what was happening. I was in the back part of the room, along with two of my friends, so I fell to the floor before the killers got close to us.

I think I was wounded when I fell to the floor. From there, I could hear the murderers, who were advancing slowly, stopping in front of each one of my friends, to shoot them dead at close range. They fired, advanced, and repeated *"Allāhu akbar"* before taking another step and another shot. It was a massacre, directed in a very precise way to each member of our team. Only four of us who were in the room survived, and I have asked myself why. Three of us were wounded and played dead: we were awake and conscious, but we remained immobile. At that moment, I thought that the killers were not professionals, because it didn't occur to them to shoot us again to be sure that no one got out of there alive. But they did kill others, among them Tignous, who had always defended minorities and poor people from the margins and who never found out that it was two of them who killed him.

I thought of the symbolism of that room: on one side, we had a group of journalists and caricature artists immersed in an intense and democratic debate about society and politics; on the other side, two young men who only knew how to use bullets and two words—"*Allāhu akbar*"—to express their ideas, if you can call them ideas.

The next day, the international press talked a lot about freedom of expression, and some critics opined that *Charlie* had gone too far in its caricatures of the Prophet Muhammad, although, in fact, the newspaper had not devoted more than six covers to the Prophet over a period of ten years. We now know, after the other terrorist attacks in France, that the problem is not about the Prophet or about the caricatures: it is about an attack against a democratic way of living and thinking.

Others, in France and in the United States, opined that it was necessary to establish limits to the freedom of expression. But what we understood the day of the attack on *Charlie*—and what was confirmed in later attacks—is that freedom of expression is the first of freedoms. In other words, we cannot think of other freedoms or understand how to organize them if we cannot speak freely about them. And this ceases to be possible if we think that in certain uncomfortable cases, freedom of expression goes "too far," since who decides, and how do you decide on the limits of what is permissible? In a horrible way, the killers reminded us that all freedoms are connected, and the first of these is freedom of expression. There was a coherence—although terrible and bloody—in their way of acting: they began at the *Charlie* offices, with a deadly attack against freedom of expression, which is the first of freedoms, and then, on November 13, at the Bataclan and at the cafés, they attacked another one of the fundamental freedoms, the freedom of association, the possibility of peacefully meeting with whomever you like. Because of that, I believe there is a direct link, not just a political one but also an existential one, between the two attacks. The attack on *Charlie* served to clear the path to that second attack against peaceful gathering.

MARIO VARGAS LLOSA: I am in complete agreement: I also believe it is a freedom on which all other freedoms depend. When the freedom of expression disappears, all other freedoms are threatened. That gives power to a weapon to silence criticism and to impose a certain type of behavior. The only defense society has to face abuses of power is the freedom of expression. That freedom is the only guarantee that other freedoms can exist in a society.

RUBÉN GALLO: Mario, days after the attack on *Charlie Hebdo*, you published an article in *El País* about terrorism, which is a subject that you've dealt with in many of your novels, although always in the Latin American context. Where were you when you found out about that attack? What was your initial reaction?

MVLL: The day of the attacks, I was in Madrid. I immediately thought of my friends in Paris, many journalists among them.

The first thing I felt was horror at such a tragedy. Later, I thought of the extraordinary paradox of that happening in the city that had invented the modern concepts of freedom, of tolerance, of coexistence in diversity. I thought of all those journalists at *Charlie Hebdo*, that ferociously funny magazine, who were in the vanguard of freedom of expression, because their work was irreverent—and irreverence is one of the greatest conquests of civilization, one of the greatest achievements of democracy, which has cost us many battles.

So on the one hand, we have the democracy that allows an irreverent freedom of expression and, on the other, two fanatics armed with machine guns who kill a team of journalists solely because in their work, they have used that freedom that is one of the most important achievements of culture. It would be a great mistake to think that attack was something exceptional, without precedent, because, in fact, the barbarism and violence that fanaticism relies on are probably the oldest traditions in humanity. Our history is full of this kind of fanatic, convinced that his truth is the only acceptable one and willing to kill anyone who contradicts him. It is a very ancient tradition, and history is full of corpses and blood because this has been a constant practice since the beginning. An important difference is that in the past we were dealing with religious dogma and in modern times what is at play is a political ideology, although in this type of terrorism ideology and religion come together. The only thing that has changed are the weapons. In the past fanatics had limited capacity to destroy because their weapons were not as efficient as ours. Nowadays machine guns and explosives can produce massacres like the ones that happened in the attacks at Atocha in Madrid, at the Bataclan in Paris, or at the Twin

Towers in New York. This is one of the main reasons to be worried. The proliferation of weapons that get more and more destructive and more efficient in their homicidal objectives is such that the type of destruction fanatics can cause is practically unlimited.

But what should we do? Of course, we have to defend ourselves. There is no doubt that we need to defend civilization against barbarism. But it is very important that our defense of civilization not attack the achievements of democracy, because then we would be unconsciously contributing to the destruction of civilization for which terrorists long. And this is something that can happen if, for example, we start to impose limits on freedom of expression because we consider it one of the necessary sacrifices that we have to make to defend our society. As Philippe pointed out, there are people who opined that *Charlie Hebdo* had no right to mock religion, to ridicule the Prophet in a caricature. But if we allow ourselves to be convinced by this kind of argument, we would end up accepting censorship and that would destroy one of the most important conquests of our society.

Censorship is the beginning of any dictatorship, of any type of totalitarian regime, because it leads to the disappearance of a spirit of criticism. In democratic societies, censorship is unnecessary because there are mechanisms to decide the few cases in which freedom of expression breaks the law: judicial power exists to penalize those abuses within a legal framework. Democracy means living politics in a civic manner. I believe that one of the most dangerous consequences of terrorism is that it can lead us, unintentionally, to destroy that great conquest of civilization.

We should not accept the terrorist's rules of the game. We

should not accept the idea that certain subjects are at the margins of freedom of expression. I believe it is something truly important today, when we are facing this exceptional terrorism. It's very important to resist the temptation of thinking that to defend freedom we have to sacrifice a degree of freedom, particularly when we're dealing with freedom of expression. It's a consideration we should have in mind after experiences like the one Philippe has described so emotionally.

PL: I'll remind you that *Charlie Hebdo* is a satirical weekly that comes from a very old French tradition. From the end of the eighteenth century, at least, France has had violent and entertaining caricaturists who mock all powers, including the Catholic religion and political personalities. The nineteenth century produced caricatures of all kinds of characters representing power. It included truly aggressive satires, with a very specific sense of humor that blends poor taste with the irony that in French we call *le second degré*. So *Charlie* belongs to that tradition. After the attacks, I heard some people and writers say that the magazine's caricatures were bad; those people made a moral judgment without knowing the tradition of French satire. I don't know if some of those caricatures were bad—that's just a question of taste—but what I do know is that individual taste cannot be used to limit freedom of expression.

RG: Philippe, can you talk to us about the misunderstandings that happened abroad over what *Charlie* was doing? I'm thinking of some statements by Joyce Carol Oates, by PEN, and by other intellectuals in the United States, who argued that the magazine had issued a frontal attack on Muslim sensitivities.

PL: It would be important to remember that *Charlie Hebdo* was criticized going back to 2006, when it published the caricatures of the Prophet from the Danish newspaper *Jyllands-Posten*. I recall a discussion I had with Charb at the time: he told me that the greater part of those caricatures seemed bad to him but that we had to publish them because it was a question of principle. There were caricaturists receiving death threats for having drawn the Prophet, and we had to support them. We had a very clear idea that we could not function as the arbiters of good taste, but we could as defenders of freedom of expression.

After the attack, very harsh criticism emerged, saying we didn't have the right to mock the Prophet, because that was an attack against the poor Muslims who already, in and of themselves, were the wretched of the earth. We were accused of being racist, which is absurd, because *Charlie Hebdo* was founded in 1970 as an absolutely anti-racist publication, against colonialism and the war in Algeria.

I understand that there was some confusion abroad because the culture of the French caricature, as I have said, is very specific and, as such, almost impossible to export. After the *Charlie* massacre, the great circulation of the magazine through the internet has increased the misunderstandings. Overnight, that very French magazine, which was loyally read by a small minority of French people, became famous the world over and now reaches millions of readers in all countries—and many times, people can't understand the humor because they're not familiar with the tradition of French caricature. They emit moral judgment about the caricatures they see on a screen, amputated from their social and political context, and frequently falsified by Islamist charlatans. We, *Charlie*'s survivors, now see how our work is read by people who absolutely don't understand the dark humor or the irony. We make jokes, but there are many people who don't laugh and who think we should stop "insulting" Islam and the Prophet. But if *Charlie* stops laughing at all of that, it will cease to be *Charlie*.

MVLL: I think it is practically impossible to write without offending someone. If a writer is free when he writes, his literature will irritate certain readers. This is inevitable if the writer freely expresses his emotions, his fantasies, his goals. The important thing is that readers understand that in a democracy there are occasions on which we feel irritated and furious with what we read. The price we pay for freedom is to see ourselves forced to read things that are unacceptable and repugnant to our view of the world. But that is what the culture of freedom and civilization is about. It is something that didn't exist in the past. Little by little, we've educated ourselves to accept the difference, a difference that can come to be repellent to our beliefs and our view of morals and ethics.

But in a democracy, we all have the right to be different from others in our usage, beliefs, and habits. And this civilized manner of cohabitating despite differences is precisely what fanatics want to destroy.

I think that the reaction of the French following the attack on *Charlie Hebdo* was fantastic: a small magazine with a small readership on the verge of bankruptcy became, overnight, a large-circulation publication with international reach.

PL: Yes. Before the attack, we had thirty thousand readers and we now have two hundred thousand. The first edition after the attack had a run of four million.

MVLL: It was a fantastic reaction on the part of the French. They want to destroy *Charlie Hebdo*? Then let's all go buy that magazine, even if we don't like it. In other words, we're going to defend democracy, the right to be irreverent, the right to feel uncomfortable with what we read. That is the true democratic spirit. The terrorists who acted in November 2015 wanted to destroy people's right to listen to music that is incompatible with religious fanaticism and the right to gather on the terraces of bars to have a drink with friends. And the reaction there was also fantastic: the bistros filled up even more with people, with millions of French people going to the terraces of bars and cafés to defend that right to assembly. That is exactly the kind of reaction we should have— reaffirming our rights—when barbarous acts of this nature occur.

We also have to think of the importance of those attacks occurring in Paris, in that city that for many of us has been a myth. For the writers of my generation, Paris was always the capital of freedom, of creativity, of art and literature, of big ideas. Paris was, in addition, the main setting for the French Revolution, which produced a political philosophy of democracy and diversity. By attacking Paris, the terrorists wanted to destroy that entire tradition of freedom, diversity, and tolerance that has been one of the greatest achievements of civilization. We should defend that democratic tradition opposing terrorism, not just through efficient policy but also by protecting the culture of tolerance.

RG: In the face of the reality of terrorist threats, one of the great debates, especially in France and in other European countries, has revolved around the need to limit certain freedoms for an indefinite period of time. In France, for example,

President Hollande activated emergency measures following the attack on *Charlie Hebdo* that allow the government to spy on any suspect. These measures have generated protests because they impinge on individual guarantees. To what point is it desirable to temporarily sacrifice freedoms in the name of security?

MVLL: It's a very complex situation because we are at war. It is a war very different from previous ones, but not any less real for that. A situation of war always carries along certain limitations of the guarantees that a democracy offers, and the great challenge is to define what the limit is. But we should be very conscious of the implicit risk of that situation of war, in which fear can lead us to sacrifice a part of those guarantees. It's a very dangerous situation because it implies the destruction of one of the most important achievements of civilization, and that is something that is already the beginning of a dictatorship. All dictatorships suppress individual freedoms in the name of peace, order, safety, stability, for the citizens' protection.

RG: I would like to talk about humor, which has played a very important role in this debate. *Charlie Hebdo* is a humoristic weekly and comes from the premise that what is at play right now is the right to be able to laugh at everything. That is also part of democracy: the idea that no person or idea is exempt from laughter, humor, satire.

PL: Yes, humor has had a very important role even after the attacks. I'd like to share an anecdote. After the attack on *Charlie*, they took me to the hospital, they sedated me, and I entered the operating room. When I awoke, something very curious happened: I felt very calm and I realized that in the face of so much violence, the only possible response was humor, curiosity, friendship, and tenderness.

Ten days after the first operation, I had a visit from President François Hollande. I received him standing, and we spoke in a very normal, very casual way, almost as if we were having a casual chat. I told him about the attack: I spoke very calmly, describing it as if it were a distant scene, and tried to show the efficient and absurd way in which the killers had acted. At that moment, my jaw and lips were still destroyed and I was making a lot of effort to speak—to speak and not drool. I felt very proud, like a child, at seeing I was managing it: each well-pronounced and measured word gave all of us, in that room, a certain dignity, a degree of civilization. And while I told the president all of this, the nurses joked and said I was a real talker, that in my state I should be more discreet.

At that moment, I realized that I was experiencing something that the killers would never be able to change: the way in which we French know how to laugh at everything, even the great tragedies. Many people imagine that we victims of terrorism fall into an inferno like the one Hieronymus Bosch painted, but the reality is very different: we fall into a purgatory in which humor, conversation, delicacy, and beauty still exist.

That day, I couldn't laugh or even smile—due to the state of my body—but for me, it was very important to make others laugh or at least smile. I felt that their smiles were a reflection of mine, as if I had lent mine to them, and it was also an act of resistance against those who want to erase the smiles from all of our faces.

I was still standing, facing the president, maintaining

that chat—and I made an effort to be as civilized as my lips allowed—in the company of my surgeon.

"We're not here to cry or feel sorry for ourselves," I told the president as lightly as possible. I saw the hint of a small smile, as if that were obvious, and he responded, "Yes. All of this has to be lived with dignity." My surgeon was standing and looking at him with an insolent smile.

The president spent forty minutes in my room, talking with me and my surgeon, who is a young, beautiful, very intelligent woman, who in addition to being an excellent doctor had a great sense of humor. Hollande was seduced by her—I realized it by the way he looked at her—and I would have liked to smile, thinking that even after an attack, in a hospital room, seduction continues to be possible and that the president continues to be a seductive man.

I looked at him again: he was wearing a simple and elegant suit, and there was something about him that did not look like his televised image. Months later, I ran into him at a public event. He recognized me immediately and came up to me. He asked me if I was better and then with a smile on his lips said, "And how's the surgeon? Do you still see her?" I responded, "Of course, and I will have to keep seeing her for a long time." He looked at me and said, "You're so lucky!"

When I told this anecdote, some of my friends seemed indignant over the president's supposed frivolity. Couldn't he think of anything else? I don't agree with them. It was very funny to me that he asked about the surgeon. That's life: happy and full of surprises. I thought that those friends don't think like novelists. To me, it seemed logical that when he saw me, he would remember the two things that most left an impression on him in that hospital room: my body and my surgeon's body. The wounded one, knowledge, and beauty: all united and struggling so that the person I was at that moment would stop being a victim, to rebuild and repair it. That is all.

I developed a very important relationship with my surgeon. We frequently spoke of literature and music. I gave her Raymond Chandler novels, because that writer has a lot of style and humor, and also because I would have liked to have lived those months like Philip Marlowe, although perhaps without so much whiskey. Now—ten months after the attack—I am still in contact with her, not only because she spent fourteen continuous hours operating on my face and then did so again many more times, but because she is intelligent and she was the one who made it possible for me to travel to Princeton to be in conversation with Mario Vargas Llosa. To date, I've had thirteen operations and I'm not done yet. More are needed to rebuild my face and my mouth, which are acts of surgery and of civilization. And when I recover my smile, I will have the power to make the killer disappear forever, as if we were in a comic book.

STUDENT: I wanted to ask you about how responses to violence can generate, in some cases, ways of symbolic violence. I'm thinking, for example, of how after September 11, intelligence agencies in the United States have been spying on citizens' conversations.

PL: This is a very emotional moment in France, because we want to find a way to defend freedom. Safety has become a primordial subject, because we can't even think about freedom if we don't live in a safe place, sheltered from violence. And what terrorists want is for us to stop thinking. That is why the French president's initial response—like that of the American president after September 11—was to increase security. During the four and a half months that I spent at the hospital, I was under police protection twenty-four hours a day. I spoke a lot with those police officers, and some of them would tell me that surely new attacks were to come and that they couldn't do anything to avoid them, because we live in a space of freedom where the police cannot arrest suspects if they haven't committed a crime. In other words, our laws only allow the arrest of terrorists when it's too late. So then, what can we do? That is a very, very complicated question. That is the problem with terrorism. What to do when our freedom, our way of life, our cell phones are what allow terrorists to act against us and attack our society? Are we willing to put limits on some of our freedoms? But what freedoms are we willing to sacrifice, and who is in charge of deciding and controlling that? Are we willing to fight? But where, against whom, and with what means? Of course, I would not like for our freedom to be limited by what happened, because that is exactly what the terrorist wants. I do not want to sacrifice our freedoms out of fear. Terrorists use bloody means to remind us that we live in an imperfect world, and that democracy implies picking the lesser of two evils. They want a very different world, which for them is a perfect world. But that world has a name, and it is called hell.

MVLL: A democratic society must defend itself against terrorism without a doubt. Terrorists should be pursued, judged, and punished with sentences that the law provides for the crimes they have committed. There also have to be certain measures taken that in times of peace would be unacceptable but that come to be unavoidable during war. Democratic countries should defend themselves by attacking the sources of terrorism.

This is what is happening now with the Islamic State, which is the territory where terrorists are trained, prepared, and armed. Is it legitimate for the Western world to attack the source of terrorism? I think so. The Islamic State is the source of almost all of this barbarism, and Western countries should attack the root of terrorism. In addition, as I said before, the great majority of the victims of terrorism are Muslim, so liberating the world of terrorism would improve the lives of Muslims. When we see what is happening in Iraq, for example, thousands and thousands of Iraqis are killed every week by terrorists. The Western world has the moral obligation to defend itself by attacking the source of terrorism, which in this case is a precise location. We know where it is, we know where the terrorists who are trying to destroy civilization come from. I believe that if we don't efficiently defend ourselves, the number of massacres will multiply and turn into violence of a kind previously unseen in history, if we consider the weapons and technology that exist today.

STUDENT: Continuing with the subject of the Islamic State, could you talk to us about Syria and the way in which Europe, the United States, and Russia have involved themselves in that war?

MVLL: That is a very good question. My impression is that the Western world, in particular the United States, made a mistake when it didn't help the opposition rebelling against Assad from the start. At the beginning, it was a democratic resistance, a popular revolution against a brutal dictator. The Western world—with the exception of France—committed a big mistake when it didn't take part in that conflict. We had the moral obligation to help those citizens who wanted to transform Syria into a democratic society. But we didn't do so, and then the members of the opposition were plowed down by terrorists, and the Islamic State came to be the main player in the battle against Assad. A very confusing situation has been created now in which Putin is made out to be the enemy of the terrorists, although we know that Russia has other interests. Putin wants to keep Assad in power so that Syria continues to be a country subordinate to Russia, in part because the Syrian government has bought weapons from it for many years. We've reached a very confusing situation in which the Western world has to decide if it ends up allying itself with Putin, although France, the United States, and Russia have such different purposes in their battle against the Islamic State.

My impression is that if we believe in the culture of freedom and in the extraordinary progress that it has meant for democratic countries, we have the moral obligation to help the movements or political parties that seek to create a democratic system such as ours in their countries. It is a way of defending the institutions of civilization. It has to be said: Assad is a dictator who rapes, every day, the rights of his citizens. To support the Syrians who want a democracy is also a way of fighting against terrorism and promoting democratic values.

But we can be optimists. My conviction is that Islamist terrorism today will never win the war it has waged against civilization. We're dealing with small minorities who are so barbarous, so fanatical, that they will always be rejected by the majority of society, not only in Western countries but also in Asian and Middle Eastern countries, which are the ones most affected by Islamist terrorism.

HISTORY AND LITERATURE

I began teaching literature when I was still a student, in 1955, at the Universidad de San Marcos. I was in my third year of literature when the Peruvian literature teacher Augusto Tamayo Vargas named me his assistant. He tasked me with teaching that subject in a summer course that San Marcos offered to foreign students, and the following year I had to lecture for one of the three hours that Professor Tamayo Vargas devoted to his course. Although I spent a lot of time preparing for the classes and ended up with quite a few gray hairs as a result, I enjoyed teaching them from the start. Suddenly, I discovered that the way one reads literature to later teach it is very different from the reading one does for pure pleasure. To teach what a poetry book, a novel, or an essay contains, you have to do a much more rational reading, and translate feelings and emotions into concepts. But, at the same time, that academic reading allows a better understanding of the influence good books have on life, how thanks to them one comes to know the language in which one expresses himself much better and learns to speak with more precision, more nuance; to imagine and dream; and to move with ease in imaginary worlds.

Following that experience, I taught for many years in England and the United States—I still do so—and it has always been a very rich and instructive intellectual adventure, in which I have learned much about my job as a writer and about the fundamental importance that books have not just in shaping people culturally but also in what it means to be a free and responsible citizen. I am convinced, for example, that a critical spirit, indispensable for a democracy to function, is shaped and enriched thanks to literature more than any other discipline.

To give this class at Princeton along with my friend Rubén Gallo was a special pleasure. The subject was my own novels, especially those with a material basis in history and politics. We divided the work in a complementary way. I spoke as an author, and he as a critic. There were two perspectives, one in which I explained the sources that had served me in writing those stories, the liberties I had taken with events and real characters, and the other in which Rubén pointed out the significance that those novels could have once they made contact with readers and went on to have lives completely independent of their author. The students' participation was the priority. Not only had the students rigorously read the novels, but in addition they had reviewed the manuscripts and notes I took as I wrote, which were in Princeton's archives. For me, it was a surprise to frequently engage in presentations in which the students knew much more than I myself did about the process of developing my fictions and were better prepared than I was to make a distinction between what in them was historical truth and what was literary invention.

Courses at Princeton are small, generally of a maximum of twenty enrolled students and two or three auditors, so that all participate in a very active way. A good part of the classes are dialogues in which students have as creative a role as the professor himself. I am not exaggerating one bit if I say that in these classes, I have learned more about my own work than the students themselves who attended them.

I have to point out in a very significant way the admirable work that Rubén Gallo has carried out with this book. He gives very faithful testimony of the content of this course, of the ideas and debates that were part of it, and, at the same time, has done very inventive and personal work. The reality was much more disordered and chaotic, but he knew how to extract from it what was most important and give it the shape of some essays that follow one after another in a harmonious and necessary way, illuminating each one of the stories with anecdotal and artisanal material that extraordinarily enriches the understanding of the novels and their historical context. In this way, the book slowly reveals, in all its complexity and nuances, that curious relationship between literature and history. Although, often, the former distances itself from events as they occurred and cuts or extends them to imbue them with more emotion, these infidelities, rather than distorting historical facts, highlight what is intense and meaningful about them, making the readers experience the story along with the main characters. To make history come alive is not something that even the best historians always manage, often stratified by the abundance of materials with which they must document their relationships and information. That is why, perhaps, the Napoleonic battles in Russia seem more authentic when Tolstoy writes them in *War and Peace*, as does the battle of Waterloo when Victor Hugo refers to it in *Les Misérables*, than when they are told, with documentary rigor, by good historians. Without the latter, novelists would not have been able to rely on history as fodder for imagination, but it is possible that without the treatments novelists have given to history, the characters and historic facts would not have the vitality and presence that they have in the lives of nations.

MARIO VARGAS LLOSA

MADRID, JULY 6, 2017

ACKNOWLEDGMENTS

We are grateful to the students of Princeton who participated in our seminar during the fall of 2015: Alexandra Aparicio, Kyle Berlin, Pablo Gutiérrez, Marlis Hinckley, Ben Hummel, Erin Lynch, Emilio Moreno, Victoria Navarro, Diego Negrón-Reichard, Lara Norgaard, Jennifer Shyue, Jorge Silva Tapia, Arón Villareal, Diego Vives, and Charlotte Williams. Thank you as well to Doctor Miguel Caballero-Vázquez, who in 2015 was studying for his doctorate at Princeton and served as teaching assistant in the seminar Literature and Politics in the Work of Mario Vargas Llosa.